# The Heart of Wisdom

## Biblical Studies, Volume 1

Sister Felicity Rivera

Published by Graywolf Press, 2025.

THE HEART OF WISDOM

**First edition. April 9, 2025.**

Copyright © 2025 Sister Felicity Rivera.

ISBN: 979-8227827555

Written by Sister Felicity Rivera.

# Table of Contents

# Chapter 1: Introduction to Wisdom Literature

Wisdom literature in the Bible has long been celebrated for its rich insights into human nature and divine truth. This opening chapter sets the stage for our in-depth study of Proverbs 3, a passage revered for its profound guidance and practical wisdom. In this chapter, we explore the concept of biblical wisdom, examine the unique characteristics of the wisdom literature genre, and explain why Proverbs 3 occupies such a central place in the canon of ancient texts. Our goal is to foster both personal and spiritual growth by inviting readers to journey through historical context, literary analysis, and reflective application.

## Purpose & Scope

At its core, wisdom literature is concerned with offering discernment and instruction for living a life that is fulfilling, meaningful, and aligned with divine principles. In the biblical tradition, wisdom is not merely an accumulation of knowledge but a way of life that transforms the heart and mind. Proverbs 3, in particular, encapsulates this transformative power by providing a roadmap for trusting in God, embracing humility, and discovering the rewards of wisdom.

### The Transformative Power of Wisdom

Wisdom as presented in the Bible is a gift from God—a guiding light meant to illuminate the path of righteousness in a complex and often confusing world. Unlike secular definitions of wisdom, which sometimes emphasize intellectual prowess or worldly success, biblical wisdom calls for a deep-rooted understanding of life that intertwines practical insight with spiritual truth. This understanding forms the foundation of a relationship with God, one that nurtures virtues such as trust, integrity, and humility.

Proverbs 3 stands as an exemplary text within this tradition. It directs believers not only to acquire knowledge but also to act on it, integrating ethical living into daily routines. The text assures us that wisdom leads to a balanced life, where every decision is informed by the compassion and righteousness that come from divine instruction. By studying Proverbs 3, readers are encouraged to reflect on their own lives, consider the areas in which they might grow, and cultivate habits that lead to both spiritual fulfillment and worldly benefits.

## Objectives of This Study Guide

The study guide accompanying this chapter is designed to move beyond a mere academic analysis. It is crafted as a resource for personal transformation, structured to nurture spiritual growth through thoughtful reflection and practical application. As you progress through this guide, you will be invited to examine profound questions, participate in guided meditations, and consider how the timeless wisdom of Proverbs can be interwoven with the modern challenges of everyday life.

Specifically, this chapter aims to:

- Introduce the Concept of Biblical Wisdom: We begin by exploring what wisdom means within a biblical framework, contrasting it with other philosophical or secular interpretations.

- Highlight the Centrality of Proverbs 3: By unpacking the themes and promises embedded in this particular chapter, we illustrate its pivotal role in encouraging trust in God and offering a blueprint for a well-lived life.

- Establish the Historical and Cultural Context: Understanding the world in which Proverbs was written enriches our interpretation. The guide delves into the background of ancient Israelite society and the role that wisdom literature played in everyday life.

- Provide a Roadmap for the Study: The chapter outlines the structure of the guide, detailing how subsequent sections will build on these foundational insights to provide a comprehensive understanding of wisdom literature.

Through these objectives, this chapter sets the tone for an explorative journey where theological insights meet practical living. It is intended not only to inform but also to inspire, encouraging you to view the teachings of Proverbs through a transformative lens.

# Overview of Proverbs

The Book of Proverbs stands among the most widely recognized portions of biblical literature, revered for its practical advice and spiritual depth. As we embark on a detailed study of Proverbs 3, it is essential to appreciate the wider context of the entire book, understanding its origins, authorship, and enduring relevance.

## A Brief History of Wisdom Literature within the Bible

Wisdom literature, as a genre, reflects humanity's enduring quest to understand the world, make sense of suffering, and pursue a good life. In the Bible, wisdom is portrayed as a divine attribute—a gift that equips human beings to navigate the complexities of existence with clarity and purpose. Proverbs, along with books like Job, Ecclesiastes, and Psalms, forms a critical subset of biblical writings that address fundamental questions about life, morality, and the nature of God.

### Origins and Development

The origins of Proverbs can be traced back to an oral tradition. In ancient Israel, wisdom was often passed down through spoken sayings, anecdotes, and parables that encapsulated life's lessons in a pithy, memorable manner. Over time, these sayings were collected, edited, and eventually written down to form what we now recognize as the Book of Proverbs. This process of compilation reflects the communal desire to preserve valuable insights and ensure their transmission to future generations.

The final form of Proverbs reflects contributions from various authors and time periods. While King Solomon is traditionally credited as the primary source of many proverbs—a testament to his legendary wisdom—scholarly research suggests that the book is a mosaic of sayings from different eras, each influenced by the cultural and spiritual milieu of its time. This layered authorship enriches Proverbs, offering multiple perspectives on what it means to live wisely.

### The Role of Wisdom in Ancient Israel

In ancient Israel, wisdom was not an abstract concept reserved for the elite; it was a practical tool for everyday life. The community valued wisdom for its ability to guide decisions, strengthen social bonds, and foster harmonious living. In a world marked by uncertainty, where the natural and divine were closely intertwined, wisdom provided comfort and clarity. The proverbs served as a moral compass, reminding individuals of their responsibilities towards both their neighbors and their God.

Wisdom literature functioned as both a personal and communal resource. For individuals, it offered guidance on personal conduct and spiritual discipline. For the community, it was a means to articulate shared values and ideals, establishing a common ethical framework. Understanding this dual role of wisdom literature helps modern readers appreciate the depth and practical orientation of Proverbs, especially in chapters like Proverbs 3, where the emphasis on personal trust in God is intertwined with communal ethical imperatives.

# Authorship, Audience, and Historical Context of Proverbs

The multifaceted nature of Proverbs is enriched by its varied authorship, expansive audience, and the historical conditions that influenced its composition. Each of these factors plays a crucial role in how the text is understood and applied even in contemporary settings.

## Authorship

Traditionally, King Solomon is regarded as the principal figure behind Proverbs, attributed with unparalleled wisdom and a flourishing court that sought to guide his subjects through sagacious counsel. Solomon's reputation as the wisest of kings, combined with his historical and literary legacy, has led many to view his contributions as foundational. However, the Book of Proverbs is not solely the work of one man. It also contains contributions from other wise individuals and scribes who compiled and edited these sayings, ensuring that the wisdom of various traditions was captured in one enduring collection.

This multiplicity of voices invites readers to see wisdom not as a singular, monolithic doctrine but as a dynamic conversation that has developed over time. It encourages modern readers to engage with these teachings as part of a long line of thoughtful inquiry, one that extends from the ancient world to the present day.

## Audience

The intended audience for Proverbs was broad. While it offers guidance that is particularly useful for young people learning the ways of life, its insights are equally applicable to seasoned adults. The text assumes that its readers seek to live in a way that is both pleasing to God and beneficial to society. It provides practical instructions on topics ranging from personal integrity and ethical behavior to the management of relationships and resources.

For contemporary readers, this inclusive approach is particularly resonant. In an era marked by a multitude of competing worldviews, the universal appeal of wisdom speaks to a fundamental human desire to live well. Whether one is a student of theology, a seeker of practical life advice, or someone on a personal spiritual journey, the teachings of Proverbs offer valuable insights that transcend time and culture.

## Historical Context

To fully appreciate the wisdom embedded in Proverbs, one must consider the historical and cultural context in which it was written. Ancient Israel was a society steeped in tradition, where the boundaries between the sacred and the mundane were fluid. Daily life was punctuated by an awareness of the divine presence, and individuals naturally sought guidance in the interpretation of life's events. This context of pervasive religiosity and communal interdependence greatly influenced the content and form of wisdom literature.

The proverbs reflect a world that was as concerned with practical matters—such as family relationships, leadership, and community welfare—as it was with abstract theological concepts. For example, the admonitions to trust in God and to honor wisdom were not merely spiritual exercises but strategies for survival and prosperity in an unpredictable environment. By blending pragmatic advice with spiritual truths, Proverbs provided a holistic vision of life that was both realistic and idealistic.

This duality of purpose is especially evident in Proverbs 3. Here, the call to trust in the Lord is presented not just as a matter of faith but as a practical prescription for navigating the complexities of daily existence. Trust, as outlined in this text, is an active choice that has tangible rewards—ranging from emotional resilience to material well-being. As such, the historical context of Proverbs helps modern readers see these ancient teachings as both timeless and immediately applicable.

# The Unique Features of Wisdom Literature in the Bible

Wisdom literature occupies a unique niche within the biblical canon. Unlike narrative histories or prophetic writings, wisdom texts are crafted to engage the reader in a reflective process of inquiry and self-improvement. They employ poetic language, concise aphorisms, and a series of practical exhortations that invite readers to ponder, question, and ultimately transform their ways of living.

## Poetic Structure and Literary Devices

One of the most striking aspects of Proverbs is its use of poetic structure. The text frequently employs parallelism—a literary device wherein ideas are repeated, contrasted, or expanded upon in successive lines. This rhythmic repetition not only reinforces the message but also aids memorization and meditative reflection. For many readers, these poetic qualities are what make the proverbs so accessible and profound, imparting layers of meaning with remarkable efficiency.

In addition, the language of Proverbs is imbued with metaphor and symbolism. Common images such as light and darkness, water and drought, or even the human heart itself are used to illustrate complex spiritual realities. These literary devices allow for multiple interpretations, inviting readers into a dialogue with the text where simple phrases can yield deep insights upon careful contemplation.

## Practical Instructions for Life

At its heart, wisdom literature is practical. Each proverb, whether a pithy admonition or a sweeping generalization, is designed to offer actionable advice. The wisdom found in Proverbs is not abstract philosophy but a guide to everyday behavior. From managing personal finances to nurturing relationships and fostering spiritual discipline, the text covers a broad spectrum of life's challenges.

Proverbs 3, for example, encapsulates this pragmatic approach. It outlines specific steps—such as trusting in the Lord wholeheartedly and acknowledging Him in all aspects of life—that are presented as both spiritual imperatives and practical guidelines. These instructions are not meant to be theoretical ideals but actionable principles that, when applied, promise real-life benefits. The promise of such practical rewards is a major reason why Proverbs has retained its popularity among generations of readers.

# Why Proverbs 3 Holds a Pivotal Role

Within the broader context of biblical wisdom literature, Proverbs 3 holds a particularly esteemed position. Its teachings are considered to be a microcosm of the entire wisdom tradition, distilling key principles into a succinct yet profound narrative. Several factors contribute to its centrality:

## A Call to Trust and Reverence

Proverbs 3 is renowned for its powerful exhortation to trust in the Lord with all one's heart—a theme that resonates deeply across various facets of life. This directive is both a command and a promise. It implores the reader to relinquish self-reliance, encouraging a posture of complete dependence on divine guidance. In doing so, it underscores a broader theological message: true wisdom begins with recognizing one's limitations and seeking higher, divine insight.

This call to trust is not presented as a mere abstract concept; it is intrinsically linked to practical outcomes. The passage promises that such trust will lead to stability, prosperity, and long life—a compelling incentive for believers who face the uncertainties of daily life. It is this balance of spiritual and practical benefits that endears Proverbs 3 to its readers and underscores its lasting relevance.

## Integration of Spiritual and Everyday Life

Another aspect that elevates Proverbs 3 is its seamless integration of spiritual doctrines with everyday living. The text does not demand a separation between the sacred and the mundane. Instead, it teaches that spiritual truths are meant to permeate every aspect of life—from personal relationships and work ethics to health and well-being. By advocating for a life where divine principles inform even the smallest decisions, Proverbs 3 provides a comprehensive framework for living wisely.

This holistic approach to life is one of the reasons why wisdom literature remains a perennial favorite for those seeking to harmonize their spiritual beliefs with their worldly responsibilities. The teachings of Proverbs 3 act as a bridge between the temporal and the eternal, ensuring that the pursuit of wisdom is both a personal and a communal journey.

## Universality and Timelessness

The universal appeal of Proverbs 3 lies in its timeless quality. Though composed in an ancient cultural context, the lessons it imparts are as applicable today as they were thousands of years ago. The challenges of decision-making, the quest for meaning, and the need for ethical guidance are as relevant in our modern society as they were in ancient Israel. This timeless relevance ensures that the study of Proverbs, and particularly Proverbs 3, continues to offer valuable insights to every generation, regardless of cultural or historical differences.

The enduring nature of the proverbs also speaks to the continuity of the human experience. In its concise yet profound expressions of wisdom, Proverbs 3 encapsulates the essence of human life—its challenges, its beauty, and its potential for transformation. This universality is a key reason why the chapter occupies such an important place in both historical and contemporary religious study.

# Concluding Thoughts: The Invitation to Seek Wisdom

As we conclude this introductory chapter, it is important to reiterate the invitation extended by biblical wisdom literature. The teachings found in Proverbs, particularly in chapter 3, are not relics of an ancient past but living principles that guide us toward a better, more enriched life. They offer a path that is not merely academic but transformational, urging the reader to internalize the truths of divine wisdom and apply them in tangible ways.

The subsequent chapters of this study guide will build upon the foundations laid here. We will delve deeper into the language, context, and practical applications of Proverbs 3, fostering a greater understanding of how these timeless instructions can shape modern lives. Through reflective questions, guided meditations, and practical exercises, we aim to create a space where wisdom is not only understood but lived.

In embracing the wisdom literature of the Bible, we open ourselves up to a tradition that has been cherished for millennia—a tradition that challenges us to think deeply, live rightly, and love unconditionally. The journey ahead is both an intellectual and spiritual one, inviting each reader to discover for themselves the transformative power of embracing divine wisdom.

This chapter has sought to lay the groundwork for that journey by exploring the historical context, literary form, and spiritual significance of Proverbs. It is an introduction not merely to a book, but to a way of life—a life that seeks to marry intellectual rigor with heartfelt devotion, practical guidance with transcendent truth. As you proceed in your study, may you find that the wisdom of Proverbs 3 offers both clarity and comfort, providing answers to life's most pressing questions and a steady guide through the myriad challenges of the modern world.

In the chapters that follow, we will continue to unravel the layers of meaning within Proverbs 3, seeking to uncover the rich tapestry of insights woven into its verses. We will explore themes such as trust in God, the rewards of humility, and the transformative power of divine discipline. Each of these themes is not an abstract theological concept but a practical principle intended to be put into practice in your daily life.

Ultimately, the study of biblical wisdom is a call to a deeper, more reflective existence—a call to live not just for momentary success but for lasting fulfillment. Let this study guide be a companion on your journey toward greater understanding, a source of inspiration as you strive to incorporate the enduring principles of Proverbs into your life. In doing so, you will embark on a path of continual growth, one that bridges the gap between the ancient and the modern, the sacred and the everyday, the spiritual and the practical.

May this exploration of wisdom inspire you to seek truth in every experience, to find guidance in every decision, and to trust in the divine path set before you. As you delve into the lessons of Proverbs, remember that true wisdom is not measured by the accumulation of facts, but by the transformation of the heart and the alignment of one's life with the higher principles of love, humility, and righteousness.

In summary, this introductory chapter has provided an extensive overview of biblical wisdom literature, setting the stage for a detailed and practical study of Proverbs 3. By reflecting on the purpose and scope of wisdom literature, its historical and cultural context, and the unique contributions of Proverbs to our understanding of divine truth, you are now well-prepared to engage with the subsequent teachings. The journey toward wisdom is ongoing, and each chapter of this guide will serve as a stepping stone toward a richer, more integrated experience of spiritual growth and everyday living.

As you move forward, keep in mind that wisdom, in its truest sense, is not a destination but a continual process of learning, unlearning, and re-learning—a dynamic relationship with God that transforms every aspect of your life. Embrace the challenge, relish the insights, and allow the timeless wisdom of Proverbs 3 to illuminate your path in ways that are both profound and practical.

# Chapter 2: Historical and Cultural Context

This chapter delves into the rich tapestry of historical and cultural elements that influenced the composition of Proverbs and the broader wisdom literature of ancient Israel. Understanding this background is essential for grasping the deeper layers of meaning within Proverbs 3. In this chapter, we explore two major areas: the ancient Israelite wisdom tradition—examining the socio-political and religious landscape of the time—and the literary and theological influences that shaped these teachings. Through a close inspection of the cultural milieu and comparisons with other ancient Near Eastern texts, we uncover the roots of biblical wisdom and the enduring theological questions it raises.

## Ancient Israelite Wisdom

### Socio-Political and Religious Background

The composition of Proverbs and the broader wisdom literature in ancient Israel is inseparable from its socio-political and religious context. During the period in which these texts were developed, Israel was a nation marked by dynamic shifts in power, a strong sense of communal identity, and a pervasive acknowledgment of the divine presence in daily life.

### Political Landscape and Social Order

In the ancient Near East, and particularly in Israel, the political environment was characterized by localized leadership, the rule of kings, and the influence of tribal customs. The era of the united monarchy under kings such as David and Solomon set a precedent for centralized power, but it was also a time when wisdom was seen as a critical resource for leadership. Kings were expected not only to command armies or manage vast resources but also to exhibit personal integrity and a deep understanding of divine law.

King Solomon, traditionally associated with a significant portion of Proverbs, embodied the ideal of a ruler whose authority was complemented by divine wisdom. His reign, celebrated for its prosperity and cultural achievements, also underscored the belief that effective governance depended on an alignment with the wisdom of God. This idea established a model where wisdom was as much a tool of statecraft as it was a guide for personal conduct. In practice, the audience for wisdom literature was not confined to political elites; it extended across all segments of society. The common people, too, were encouraged to pursue wisdom as a means of maintaining social order and living in harmony within the community.

The decentralized nature of ancient Israelite society meant that communities were tightly knit, with social life centered on family, tribal affiliation, and religious observance. This interdependence fostered an environment in which wisdom, often transmitted orally before being recorded in texts, played an integral role in teaching virtues such as justice, fairness, and prudent decision-making. Everyday interactions were governed by unwritten codes derived from this wisdom tradition, making the transition from spoken word to written text a natural progression in preserving these timeless principles.

**Religious Life and Its Impact on Wisdom**

Religion was the cornerstone of ancient Israelite life. The belief in one transcendent God who was both immanent and actively involved in human affairs distinguished Israel from its polytheistic neighbors.

This monotheistic perspective fostered a unique approach to wisdom, where divine insight was linked intrinsically with moral behavior and personal integrity.

The Law—the Torah—provided the ethical framework, but wisdom literature offered a complementary perspective. While the Torah prescribed commandments and rituals, wisdom texts like Proverbs provided practical guidance for daily living, advising individuals on how to manifest their faith in concrete actions and attitudes. This blend of the legal and the ethical created a comprehensive system where obedience to divine commands was seen as a pathway to both personal well-being and communal flourishing.

Religious festivals, temple rituals, and daily prayers reinforced the centrality of God in public and private life. The pervasive sense of divine oversight encouraged ethical behavior, and the wisdom literature functioned as an accessible reminder of how to live in accordance with God's will. In Proverbs, for instance, the call to "trust in the Lord with all your heart" is not merely a spiritual command but a practical mandate that seeks to integrate faith into every aspect of life. This integration ensured that wisdom was not seen as an abstract or academic concept but as an indispensable guide for every decision, from the mundane to the monumental.

## Cultural Influences on the Teaching of Wisdom

Culture in ancient Israel was deeply interwoven with practices, traditions, and oral teachings that had been passed down through generations. These cultural influences played a significant role in shaping the teachings on wisdom that we encounter in the biblical texts.

## Oral Traditions and the Transmission of Wisdom

Before the advent of widespread literacy, oral tradition was the primary vehicle for transmitting knowledge, values, and life lessons. Proverbs, like many other wisdom texts, originated in this oral culture where storytelling, proverbs, and sayings were crafted to communicate deep truths in simple, memorable forms. The rhythmic and parallel structure of these sayings was not only aesthetically pleasing but also served as an effective mnemonic device, ensuring that important teachings could be passed on accurately from one generation to the next.

This oral foundation meant that wisdom was a living tradition—constantly evolving to meet the needs of a changing society while remaining rooted in time-tested principles. As communities transitioned from oral to written culture, these sayings were compiled and refined, ensuring that the dynamic interplay between tradition and textual preservation was maintained. This process of compilation is evident in the layered authorship of Proverbs, where multiple voices and perspectives are interwoven to create a tapestry of communal wisdom.

## Influence of Neighboring Cultures

The ancient Near East was a crossroads of different cultures and empires, each contributing to the intellectual and spiritual life of the region. Israel was not isolated from the influences of its neighbors—Babylon, Egypt, Assyria, and others all had their own traditions of wisdom literature. These texts often shared similar themes: the importance of justice, the inevitability of human suffering, and the search for a moral and ethical life.

For instance, Egyptian literature, with its focus on maat (truth, balance, and order), offered parallels to the biblical understanding of wisdom as a way to maintain cosmic and social order.Similarly, the wisdom literature of Mesopotamia, with works like the "Instructions of Shuruppak," presented advice on proper conduct and highlighted the consequences of moral failure. While the Israelite wisdom tradition was distinctly monotheistic and intimately tied to the covenant with God, it nonetheless absorbed and reinterpreted themes from these neighboring cultures, integrating them into a framework that emphasized a personal relationship with a single, sovereign deity.

This interplay of influences enriched the biblical wisdom tradition and allowed for a cross-pollination of ideas. Elements of these external cultures can be seen in the structure, style, and thematic content of Proverbs. The universal appeal of wisdom literature, regardless of its cultural origin, underscores a shared human concern with understanding life and navigating its complexities with virtue and prudence.

# Literary and Theological Influences

## Comparison with Other Ancient Near Eastern Wisdom Texts

A comparative study of wisdom literature reveals that the biblical texts, while unique in their theological assertions, share many similarities with contemporary works from the ancient Near East. Exploring these similarities and differences can provide a fuller understanding of the distinctive characteristics of Proverbs 3.

### Structural and Thematic Parallels

Many ancient cultures produced collections of proverbial sayings intended to guide personal conduct. For example, the "Instruction of Amenemope," an Egyptian wisdom text, bears a striking resemblance to several proverbs in the Bible. Both collections offer advice on how to manage interpersonal relationships, maintain social order, and live a life that is pleasing to the divine. Common themes such as the inevitability of divine justice, the benefits of ethical behavior, and the perils of folly run through these texts, suggesting a shared cultural milieu that valued wisdom as the cornerstone of a successful life.

However, while the structural similarities are notable, there are key differences in emphasis and underlying worldview. The biblical approach, and Proverbs 3 in particular, is deeply embedded in a framework of covenantal relationship with God. In this context, the promises of prosperity, long life, and protection are not merely rewards for ethical behavior but are also seen as reflections of God's commitment to His people. In contrast, while other Near Eastern texts may invoke the favor of a deity or deities, they often lack the same intimate, reciprocal relationship evident in the Hebrew scriptures.

## The Role of Divine Providence

In ancient Near Eastern wisdom texts, the capricious nature of fate and the gods is a recurring theme. However, in Proverbs, there is a clear juxtaposition of human responsibility and divine providence. The biblical text portrays wisdom as not only a desirable attribute in its own right but also as an essential means for aligning oneself with the divine order. Proverbs 3, with its emphatic injunctions to trust in God and honor Him in all ways, explicitly ties everyday decisions to the favor and protection of the Creator.

This notion of a personal, intervening God who actively shapes the destiny of His people is a significant departure from the often impersonal deities of other ancient texts. In many respects, Proverbs 3 elevates the pursuit of wisdom to an act of faith—a means by which believers can experience the tangible benefits of a lived relationship with God. This theological nuance not only sets the biblical wisdom tradition apart but also imbues its teachings with a sense of urgency and personal relevance that transcends time.

## Understanding the Theological Underpinnings in Proverbs 3

Proverbs 3 stands out not only for its practical advice but also for its rich theological content. The chapter embodies a worldview in which wisdom is seen as a vital conduit between human life and divine grace. Here, we examine the theological dimensions that run through the text and explore how they informed the broader wisdom tradition of ancient Israel.

### Trust in God as the Foundation of Wisdom

At the heart of Proverbs 3 is the exhortation to "Trust in the LORD with all your heart and lean not on your own understanding." This verse encapsulates a central tenet of the biblical worldview—that the pursuit of wisdom is inseparable from the act of trusting in God. For the ancient Israelites, who lived in a world replete with uncertainty and external threats, trust in God provided a stable anchor amid the chaos of everyday life. By relying not on their limited human insight but on divine guidance, believers were promised not only spiritual enlightenment but also tangible blessings such as security, prosperity, and longevity.

This call to trust forms the theological backbone of Proverbs 3, linking personal piety with communal well-being. It suggests that wisdom is not an abstract ideal but a practical means to engage with life in a way that is both prudent and spiritually enriching. Trust, in this context, becomes a daily exercise in faith, inviting readers to see every decision and challenge as an opportunity to reaffirm their commitment to divine principles.

## The Interplay between Divine Discipline and Human Responsibility

Another key theological element in Proverbs 3 is the concept of divine discipline. The text explains that God's corrections are not punitive in the conventional sense but are manifestations of His love—meant to steer individuals back onto the path of righteousness. This idea is embedded in the broader biblical understanding that discipline is an integral part of spiritual growth. For ancient Israelites, the experience of divine discipline was both corrective and restorative, serving as a reminder of the constant interplay between God's expectations and human imperfection.

This theological concept has significant implications for how one approaches life's challenges. It encourages a mindset in which setbacks are not seen as failures but as opportunities for learning and growth. The recognition that divine discipline is a sign of God's active involvement in daily life provides a framework for interpreting hardships as part of a larger, divinely orchestrated plan. This perspective, which finds a powerful expression in Proverbs 3, offers believers a way to navigate the complexities of life with resilience and hope.

## The Convergence of Temporal and Eternal Values

In Proverbs 3, the promises of wisdom are portrayed as both immediate and everlasting. The text reassures its readers that trust in God and adherence to divine wisdom will yield benefits in this life—such as health, prosperity, and protection—while also setting the stage for eternal rewards. This dual emphasis reflects a theology that does not compartmentalize the temporal and the eternal but sees them as intertwined dimensions of a single, coherent reality.

For ancient Israelites, whose lives were deeply embedded in the rhythms of both the agricultural cycle and religious festivals, this convergence of the temporal and the eternal was a source of immense comfort and motivation. The promises articulated in Proverbs 3 offered a blueprint for living that was directly applicable to daily struggles while simultaneously nurturing an enduring hope for redemption and restoration beyond the present life. This synthesis of worldly and transcendent values remains one of the most compelling aspects of Proverbs, inviting readers to consider how daily actions can reflect an eternal commitment to divine principles.

## A Blueprint for a Life of Holistic Flourishing

Finally, the theological underpinnings of Proverbs 3 serve as a blueprint for holistic living—one that integrates personal, social, and spiritual dimensions. The chapter invites readers into a comprehensive approach to life where practical wisdom is harmonized with a deep sense of spiritual responsibility. Every exhortation—to trust, to honor, to accept discipline—is woven into a tapestry that depicts the ideal life, one where success is measured not by material accumulation alone but by the depth of one's relationship with God.

This holistic vision was revolutionary in its time and continues to resonate today. It challenges the modern compartmentalization of life into silos such as work, leisure, and spirituality, urging a reintegration that honors the interconnectedness of all aspects of existence. For those seeking to lead a balanced, purposeful life, Proverbs 3 provides not just guidance but a transformative framework—one that encourages the simultaneous cultivation of wisdom, faith, and ethical conduct.

# Conclusion: The Enduring Legacy of Historical and Cultural Influences

The historical and cultural contexts explored in this chapter reveal that the wisdom of Proverbs did not emerge in a vacuum. Instead, it was forged in the crucible of ancient Israelite society—a milieu shaped by dynamic political structures, a fervent religious life, and a rich tapestry of cultural practices and influences. By tracing the origins of wisdom literature through its socio-political and religious background, we gain insight into how practical advice and divine guidance became intertwined in texts like Proverbs 3.

Furthermore, the literary and theological influences—evident in the similarities with and differences from other ancient Near Eastern wisdom texts—highlight the distinctive character of biblical wisdom. Proverbs 3 stands as a testament to a worldview that prizes trust in a personal God, embraces the corrective role of divine discipline, and envisions life as a harmonious blend of temporal success and eternal promise.

As you continue your study of Proverbs, it is important to remember that each proverb is embedded within this complex historical and cultural framework. The teachings in Proverbs 3 are both a product of their time and a timeless guide for living. They invite readers to engage with wisdom in a manner that is as relevant today as it was in the ancient world—a call to live with insight, integrity, and a steadfast trust in divine providence.

By understanding the background against which these texts were written, we are better equipped to appreciate the depth and nuance of their message. The wisdom literature of ancient Israel remains a rich source of insight, offering not only guidance for personal conduct but also a profound reflection of the values and beliefs that have shaped human civilization for millennia.

In summary, this chapter has unpacked the historical and cultural contexts that continue to inform our understanding of biblical wisdom. We have explored the socio-political and religious dynamics of ancient Israel, examined the cultural influences that molded its teachings, and compared these with the broader traditions of the ancient Near East. Importantly, we have seen how these factors converge in Proverbs 3 to present a vision of wisdom that is as practical as it is theological—a blueprint for holistic flourishing that bridges the gap between everyday life and the eternal promises of a divine relationship.

As you proceed to the next chapters, keep in mind the powerful legacy of these influences. They provide the foundation upon which the transformative insights of Proverbs are built, inviting each reader to discover how ancient wisdom can still illuminate our modern journey toward a life of meaning, balance, and spiritual depth.

# Chapter 3: Structure and Language of Proverbs 3

In this chapter, we delve into the intricate details of Proverbs 3 by examining its literary architecture, the specific language and terminology that shape its interpretation, and the diverse hermeneutical approaches that scholars and practitioners employ when engaging with this text. By understanding the poetic structure, the significance of key Hebrew terms, and the various methods of interpretation, readers are better equipped to appreciate the depth and nuance of Proverbs 3 and how its timeless wisdom continues to inform and guide spiritual reflection and everyday living.

## Literary Structure of Proverbs 3

### Poetic Form and Parallelism

One of the most distinctive features of Proverbs 3, as with the rest of the biblical wisdom literature, is its poetic form. Hebrew poetry, unlike its Western metrical cousins, does not rely on strict syllabic patterns or rhyme schemes. Instead, it employs parallelism—a form of repetition and variation in phrasing that enhances both the aesthetic and the mnemonic qualities of the text.

### Types of Parallelism

Scholars have identified several types of parallelism within Proverbs 3:
    - Synonymous Parallelism: In this form, two or more lines express nearly identical or reinforcing ideas. For example, a command to trust in the Lord may be restated to emphasize the certainty of divine

support. The repetition of similar notions helps embed the message in the reader's mind.

- Antithetic Parallelism: Here, contrasting ideas are set side by side to highlight differences, such as wisdom versus folly or trust versus self-reliance. This contrast is not merely stylistic; it deepens the reader's understanding by clearly delineating the choices and consequences inherent in everyday life.

- Synthetic Parallelism: This involves a progression of ideas where the second line builds upon the thought introduced in the first. In Proverbs 3, such construction often provides a cause-and-effect relationship, illustrating how particular behaviors lead to certain outcomes.

The chapter's frequent use of parallelism helps reinforce its central themes by establishing a rhythmic cadence and reinforcing the ideas through repetition. For instance, the opening verses famously encourage the reader to "not lean on your own understanding" while simultaneously insisting, "in all your ways acknowledge Him," which together guide the believer toward a life of trust and humility. This rhythmic repetition isn't only effective for memorization but also enriches the text with layers of meaning, inviting deeper reflection each time the passage is read.

## Stylistic Features Unique to Proverbs 3

Beyond parallelism, Proverbs 3 exhibits several stylistic features that contribute to its memorable impact:

### Conciseness and Aphorism

Proverbs 3 is composed largely of aphorisms—short, pointed statements that encapsulate profound truths. This conciseness is a hallmark of ancient wisdom literature, serving both as a practical guide and as a medium for reflective meditation. Each aphorism is carefully crafted to be both easy to remember and rich in meaning, ensuring that the reader can internalize the lessons in a direct and impactful way. The economy of language used in Proverbs 3 forces every word to carry significant weight, which is why even a short verse can invoke extensive theological and ethical insights.

## Use of Imperative Statements

Another characteristic of the chapter is its frequent use of imperatives—direct commands that guide behavior. This stylistic approach underscores the urgency and importance of the teachings. Phrases such as "Trust in the LORD with all your heart" and "Do not be wise in your own eyes" are not presented as suggestions but as mandates for proper living. The imperatives are designed to provoke a sense of immediacy in the listener, urging an active response rather than passive contemplation.

## Imagery and Metaphor

Proverbs 3 makes extensive use of imagery and metaphor to evoke vivid mental pictures that convey abstract spiritual truths. Such imagery—like light and darkness, or pathways and roads—serves to illustrate the journey of life and the choices one must make. For example, wisdom is often compared to a guiding light that illuminates one's path, an image that resonates across cultures and epochs. These metaphors allow the text to be accessible even as it offers layers of symbolic meaning that invite continual re-interpretation.

## Sound Devices and Rhythm

Though modern readers might not immediately recognize the significance of sound devices in ancient Hebrew poetry, the original text of Proverbs 3 would have resonated with its audience through its rhythmical qualities. The balanced structure achieved by parallelism creates a musicality that aids in memorization and recitation. The natural cadence and pauses in the poetry of Proverbs draw attention to the turning points in thought, emphasizing the interplay between exhortation and promise.

# Language and Terminology in Proverbs 3

The language of Proverbs 3 is imbued with significance, much of which is derived from key Hebrew terms that have been the subject of extensive scholarly discussion. A deeper understanding of these terms is essential for appreciating both the literal and the metaphorical dimensions of the text.

## Defining Key Hebrew Terms

### "Chesed" – Lovingkindness or Steadfast Love

One of the terms frequently encountered in biblical literature—and implicitly present in the spirit of Proverbs 3—is *chesed*. This Hebrew word connotes a profound sense of loyalty, mercy, and steadfast love. It is a term that encapsulates not only emotional affection but also a moral commitment to act with kindness and justice. In many instances throughout the Hebrew Bible, chesed is used to describe the enduring love of God for His people—a love that remains unbroken despite human shortcomings. In Proverbs 3, the spirit of chesed can be seen in the call to honor God in all aspects of life, suggesting that the relationship between the believer and the divine is characterized by deep, enduring loyalty and benevolence.

# "Da'at" – Knowledge and Understanding

Another essential term is da'at, often translated as knowledge. However, in the context of Proverbs 3, da'at carries a broader connotation that includes discernment, understanding, and an experiential wisdom that transforms the individual from within. Unlike mere factual knowledge, da'at is about perceiving the underlying principles of life and living in accordance with divine truth. It involves both an intellectual and a spiritual dimension. The admonition "Do not be wise in your own eyes" implicitly warns against an overreliance on superficial, human knowledge at the expense of true, God-given insight (da'at). The holistic concept of knowledge proposed in Proverbs encourages the reader to pursue a wisdom that enriches the spirit, aligning the intellect with the heart.

## Other Significant Terms and Their Nuances

-"Emunah" (Faithfulness/Trust): While Proverbs 3 famously exhorts trust in the Lord, the underlying concept is emunah, a term denoting both loyalty and a steadfast commitment to God. This dual aspect of trust—as both an emotional and ethical stance—underscores the biblical call to live a life grounded in relational fidelity with the divine.

- "Yirah" (Reverence/Fear):Often translated as fear, yirah in a biblical context implies a profound reverence and awe toward God, a recognition of His majesty that leads to ethical living. This reverential fear serves as the starting point for acquiring wisdom, as it directs the individual to a humble posture before God.

- "Tov" (Good): The notion of goodness in Proverbs is rich and multifaceted. It is not simply a moral quality but encompasses wholeness, well-being, and an alignment with the divine order. The repeated emphasis on doing good in Proverbs 3 calls the reader to a lifestyle that is in harmony with the broader cosmic order envisioned in the biblical narrative.

## Impact on Interpretation

The specific choice of terminology in Proverbs 3 is not arbitrary but is carefully calibrated to invoke a particular understanding of the relationship between human beings and the divine. The layered meanings of these Hebrew words invite multiple layers of interpretation, enriching the text and allowing it to speak to diverse audiences across time and cultures. For instance, the interplay between chesed and da'at encapsulates a vision of wisdom that is not merely intellectual but is deeply relational, rooted in the experience of God's enduring love and the responsive trust it inspires.

Understanding these terms also helps clarify the text's practical implications. When Proverbs 3 instructs the reader to "trust in the LORD with all your heart," it is not simply advocating for emotional reliance; it is urging a holistic trust that encompasses the ethical, intellectual, and spiritual dimensions of life. This comprehensive vision of wisdom requires the integration of divine love (chesed), true knowledge (da'at), steadfast faith (emunah), and reverence (yirah), culminating in a lifestyle that is characterized by balance, depth, and holistic flourishing.

# Interpretive Approaches to Proverbs 3

Given the rich literary structure and the depth of its terminology, Proverbs 3 has inspired a wide range of interpretive approaches. These methods reflect the varied interests of scholars, theologians, and lay readers who seek to understand the text both in its original context and in its application to modern life.

## Historical-Critical Approach

The historical-critical method seeks to understand Proverbs 3 within the context of its time. Proponents of this approach focus on reconstructing the historical, social, and cultural conditions of ancient Israel to illuminate the text's meaning. By examining archaeological findings, ancient Near Eastern texts, and the socio-political milieu of the period, scholars using this method attempt to uncover the original intent of the text and the circumstances under which it was written.

For example, the commands to trust in God and to avoid self-reliance can be better understood when viewed against the backdrop of a society that valued communal interdependence and recognized the precariousness of life in an often-hostile region. The historical-critical approach thus helps situate Proverbs 3 within a lived reality where divine guidance was not an abstract concept but a vital means of survival and social cohesion.

## Literary and Formalist Approaches

While the historical-critical method emphasizes external context, literary and formalist approaches focus on the internal features of the text. Scholars in this tradition analyze the poetic structure, use of parallelism, and rhetorical devices within Proverbs 3 to extract meaning. This approach pays close attention to the craftsmanship of the text—how its structure and language work together to create a unified, persuasive message.

In Proverbs 3, the literary approach reveals how the balanced construction of thoughts and the repetition of key ideas reinforce the main themes of trust, humility, and divine guidance. By dissecting the text's stylistic elements, formalist interpreters show how the rhythm, pacing, and carefully chosen metaphors create a meditative quality that encourages both reflection and action.

## Theological and Devotional Interpretations

For many readers, Proverbs 3 is not merely an academic text but a source of spiritual nourishment. Theological and devotional interpretations focus on the ways in which the text can shape personal faith and practice. This approach views Proverbs 3 as a living document that provides practical wisdom for daily living while also revealing deeper truths about the nature of God and the relationship between the divine and humankind.

Devotional interpreters often highlight the passage, "Trust in the LORD with all your heart and lean not on your own understanding," as a call to surrender one's will to God. This perspective emphasizes personal transformation, encouraging readers to move beyond self-reliance toward a deeper, more trusting relationship with the divine. The theological reading reaffirms that the promises of Proverbs 3—such as security, prosperity, and long life—are contingent on a life lived in humble dependence on God's guidance. This devotional approach is especially popular among believers seeking to integrate their spiritual practices with everyday decision-making.

## Philosophical and Ethical Readings

Another dimension of interpretive work on Proverbs 3 arises from its philosophical and ethical implications. Some scholars approach the text as a work of practical philosophy, exploring its insights into human nature, morality, and the good life. From this viewpoint, the chapter is seen as an ethical manual that delineates the virtues needed for a well-lived life.

By examining themes such as the virtues of humility, prudence, and trust, philosophical interpreters place Proverbs 3 within a broader discourse on ethics that spans different cultures and historical periods. This approach often engages with similar wisdom traditions from other ancient civilizations, drawing parallels and contrasts to highlight what makes the biblical message distinctive. The focus is on how the text's moral prescriptions can guide individual behavior and contribute to a just and balanced society.

## Integrative Approaches

In recent decades, scholars have increasingly advocated for integrative approaches that combine elements of historical-critical, literary, theological, and philosophical interpretation. Such methods recognize that Proverbs 3 functions on multiple levels simultaneously—it is at once a product of its historical context, a work of poetic artistry, a source of spiritual insight, and a guide to ethical living.

Integrative interpreters strive to weave together the insights of these various approaches to create a more comprehensive reading of the text. For instance, understanding the historical background of ancient Israel enriches a literary analysis by providing context for its stylistic choices, while theological reflections enhance the ethical implications of the text. This holistic perspective acknowledges that Proverbs 3 speaks to both the intellect and the heart, inviting its readers to a multidimensional engagement with wisdom.

# Synthesis and Reflections on Structure and Language

The examination of Proverbs 3 reveals a masterpiece of ancient wisdom literature that is carefully constructed to serve multiple functions. Its sophisticated use of poetic structure and parallelism ensures that its message is both memorable and deeply layered. The deliberate selection of key Hebrew terms such as chesed, da'at, emunah, and yirah enriches the text, allowing it to convey a vision of wisdom that integrates moral, intellectual, and spiritual dimensions.

Moreover, the varied interpretive approaches available today—ranging from historical-critical and literary to theological, devotional, and philosophical—demonstrate that Proverbs 3 is not a static relic but a living document that continues to speak to contemporary concerns. Whether one is seeking academic insights, spiritual guidance, ethical direction, or a combination of all three, the text offers resources to meet those needs.

For the modern reader, engaging with Proverbs 3 is both a challenging and rewarding endeavor. It calls for a careful, nuanced reading that appreciates the subtleties of its language and the complexities of its structure. Yet, it also offers the assurance that its ancient wisdom remains relevant. In an age marked by rapid change and uncertainty, the call to trust in a higher order—grounded in the multifaceted wisdom of Proverbs 3—provides a steadfast anchor.

In reflecting on the text's structure and language, one is invited to consider how these elements work together to create an integrated vision of the good life. Each poetic line, each carefully chosen term, contributes to a broader tapestry of meaning. This tapestry, in turn, challenges the reader to adopt a posture of humility, to seek deeper knowledge, and to live in accordance with principles that transcend the immediate and the transient.

The interdependence of literary form, language, and interpretive practice in Proverbs 3 teaches us that wisdom is not merely about accumulating information, but about cultivating an inner life that is responsive to divine truth. This holistic understanding of wisdom transcends simple intellectual exercise—it demands that we live out our knowledge through actions marked by love, trust, and ethical integrity.

## Concluding Thoughts

As we close this chapter on the structure and language of Proverbs 3, it is important to appreciate the text's enduring power. Its poetic architecture, rich with parallelism and stylistic finesse, invites readers into a deeper engagement with the words and ideas that have shaped human thought for millennia. The key Hebrew terms not only elucidate the text's original meaning but also continue to influence its interpretation today, linking contemporary readers with the ancient voices of wisdom.

Furthermore, the variety of interpretive approaches underscores that Proverbs 3 remains a dynamic field of inquiry. Whether approached as a historical artifact, a work of art, a theological guide, or a philosophical treatise, the chapter offers a wealth of insights that are both practical and profound. This multiplicity of perspectives ensures that the text remains accessible and relevant to diverse audiences, each of whom may find in it a unique source of inspiration and guidance.

In a world that often seems fragmented by competing values and information overload, the integrative vision of Proverbs 3 stands as a beacon of holistic wisdom. It reminds us that true understanding arises when we allow language, literature, and faith to converge, offering us not only an intellectual framework but also a practical roadmap for life.

Ultimately, the study of Proverbs 3's structure and language is an invitation—a call to peer beneath the surface of simple exhortations to discover the deeper, layered meanings that continue to resonate through the ages. As you continue on your journey through this study guide, may the insights gleaned from this chapter enrich your reading, inspire further reflection, and lead you to a more profound, integrated experience of wisdom.

In summary, Proverbs 3 exemplifies the power of well-crafted language and poetic form to convey timeless truths about life, ethics, and our relationship with the divine. Its rich structural features, deliberate use of language, and the myriad approaches available for its interpretation all contribute to making it a cornerstone of biblical wisdom literature. By exploring these elements in depth, we open ourselves to a fuller, more nuanced appreciation of the text—one that not only informs our minds but also transforms our hearts and actions.

Through a careful study of its literary devices and terminology, we are challenged to look beyond mere words and to seek the life-changing principles that underlie every verse. In doing so, we embrace a tradition that has guided countless generations and that continues to illuminate our path in an ever-changing world.

# Chapter 4: The Call to Trust in God

Trust in God is at the heart of the biblical message and a central theme in Proverbs 3 and other wisdom texts. In this chapter, we explore the call to trust in the Lord as an invitation to transform the inner life and daily living of believers. By examining key verses that articulate this call, unpacking the concepts of faith and trust, and offering devotional reflections with guided prayers and meditative points, we invite readers to deepen their relationship with God. This chapter is crafted not only as an academic study but also as a living resource to inspire personal transformation and spiritual growth.

## 4.1 Introduction: The Significance of Trust

Trust in God stands as a timeless, universal command that has sustained countless generations. In an ever-changing world where uncertainty and anxiety abound, the biblical call to trust offers a steadfast anchor—a promise of divine favor, guidance, and protection. When we speak of trust in God, we refer to a trust that exceeds mere intellectual assent; it is a deep, abiding reliance on God's character and promises. This trust molds our choices, influences our ethical behavior, and cultivates a resilient faith that anchors us amidst life's trials.

Throughout Scripture, trust in God is repeatedly shown not only as an abstract virtue but as a practical, tangible source of blessing. Whether in moments of joy or times of crisis, the invitation to trust is linked with a promise of renewal, protection, and even prosperity. The biblical narrative, and in particular Proverbs 3, teaches that trusting in the Lord goes far beyond wishful thinking—it requires commitment, courage, and consistent application. This chapter begins by diving into the key verses of Proverbs 3 that articulate this mandate, before examining how personal faith and obedience form the foundation of true trust, and finally offering reflective practices that help embed this truth in daily life.

# 4.2 Key Verses: The Blueprint for Divine Favor

One cannot consider the call to trust in God without examining the powerful verses that embody this message. While many passages in Scripture speak to trust and reliance on God, a few standout verses in Proverbs 3 synthesize the promise of divine favor into clear, compelling counsel.

## 4.2.1 "Trust in the LORD with all your heart..."

The famous exhortation, "Trust in the LORD with all your heart and lean not on your own understanding" (Proverbs 3:5), encapsulates the core of biblical trust. This verse is both a command and a promise. It invites believers to abandon the reliance on personal insight alone and to place complete confidence in God's wisdom. The use of "all your heart" indicates that trust is to be holistic—engaging the very center of one's emotions, decisions, and life direction.

This verse works as a foundation of the entire chapter. It invites introspection: Is my trust divided, fragmented between self-reliance and divine reliance? It prompts a re-examination of personal biases and intellect that might stand in opposition to the faithfulness of God. In essence, God is calling us to reframe our perspective—from a view that privileges human strength and insight to one that recognizes divine omniscience and care.

## 4.2.2 "In all your ways acknowledge Him..."

Continuing the theme, Proverbs 3:6 instructs: "In all your ways acknowledge Him, and He shall direct your paths." This verse reinforces that trust must manifest in every aspect of life. The word "acknowledge" suggests active recognition—not a passive nod, but a continual, deliberate recognition of God's sovereignty in every decision and direction.

The promise that "He shall direct your paths" gives substance to the command—it assures that God's guidance is not abstract or remote, but personal and immediate. When believers open themselves to divine guidance, the inevitable result is a life led by purpose and clarity, even if the journey is not always free from difficulty. The assertion here is radical: complete faith triggers a transformational process in which the divine actively participates in steering one's course.

## 4.2.3 The Interplay between Trust and Blessings

The subsequent verses in Proverbs 3 describe the tangible blessings that flow from trusting in the Lord. For instance, the text links trust with health, prosperity, and longevity. This clear causal relationship—where trust fosters divine favor—is essential because it frames trust as both a personal commitment and a practical strategy for navigating life. Divine favor in this context is not seen as a mere reward for pious conduct but as an integral aspect of a right relationship with God.

The words of Proverbs remind us that embracing trust reconfigures the believer's outlook. By submitting to divine authority and guidance, one experiences a shift in the priorities of life—from self-centered ambition to an outward focus on community, justice, and love. In this way, the call to trust is a call to transformation: an invitation to live in a state of continual openness to divine intervention and mercy.

# 4.3 Faith and Trust Defined: The Relationship between Trust, Obedience, and Personal Faith

Understanding the call to trust requires a thoughtful exploration of what faith and trust mean in a biblical sense. While the two concepts are intertwined, they have distinct nuances that together help shape the believer's relationship with God.

## 4.3.1 Defining Faith in a Biblical Context

Biblical faith is more than a belief system; it is a dynamic, living relationship with the divine. Faith is often characterized by acts of obedience, a willingness to surrender personal agendas, and an unwavering belief in the promises of God. Hebrews 11:1 famously defines faith as "the assurance of things hoped for, the conviction of things not seen." In other words, true faith involves a commitment to trust in God's unseen yet steadfast reality. This commitment is not contingent upon empirical evidence, but rests on the deep-seated conviction that God's character is immutable and benevolent.

This definition of faith underscores that trust in God naturally follows from faith. The believer's commitment is not passive; it involves actively choosing to follow God's commandments, even when the path is uncertain. Faith is thus both the seed and the fruit of trust—it begins with a belief in God's greatness and matures into an active reliance on His guidance.

## 4.3.2 Trust as Active Reliance on God

Trust differs from faith in its emphasis on action. While faith is about belief, trust is about a steadfast commitment that drives behavior. When Proverbs 3 commands believers to trust in the Lord, it is calling for an active reliance on God's care and wisdom. This means making decisions based not on the often-limited human perspective, but on a confidence that God's plan is both perfect and benevolent.

Trust in this biblical sense is comprehensive. It affects every aspect of life—personal, relational, social, and spiritual. Trust compels the believer to enter into a covenantal relationship where both obedience and dependence play key roles. Trust requires surrender: a conscious decision to let go of the illusion of control and to embrace the divine orchestration of life's events. This surrender is not a passive resignation; it is an active, intentional placing of one's whole being into God's hands.

## 4.3.3 The Role of Obedience in Trust

Obedience is a natural outgrowth of trust. When one trusts in God, obedience is no longer burdensome but becomes an expression of gratitude and respect. In biblical narratives, obedience consistently leads to blessings—whether seen in the life of Abraham, Moses, or the prophets. The promise that "He shall direct your paths" (Proverbs 3:6) is contingent on acknowledging God in all things, which is in turn the fruit of an obedient heart.

Obedience in the context of trust involves daily choices. It is not limited to grand acts of faith but is found in the routine decisions that shape one's character. Whether it is choosing honesty in a difficult conversation or exhibiting kindness during a conflict, every act of obedience reinforces trust in God's provision and grace. Thus, by obeying God's commands, we solidify our trust and allow divine favor to permeate every part of our lives.

## 4.3.4 Interconnectedness of Trust, Faith, and Obedience

The relationship between trust, faith, and obedience is synergistic. They form a virtuous cycle that undergirds the believer's experience. Faith initiates the process, trust sustains it, and obedience embodies it. This interconnectedness can be summarized as follows:

- Faith provides the foundational belief in God's reliability and the truth of His promises.

- Trust moves this belief into the realm of action, demanding that we rely on God's guidance rather than our own understanding.

- Obedience is the outward manifestation of trust and faith, a continual practice that solidifies our relationship with God.

When these elements are in harmony, they transform how we live our lives. The call to trust in God is not merely about avoiding the pitfalls of pride and self-reliance; it is about embracing a transformative relationship where every facet of our being is aligned with divine will.

# 4.4 Devotional Reflection: Guided Prayers and Meditation Points

In addition to scholarly and theological exploration, the call to trust in God invites personal devotional practice. This section provides guided prayers and meditation points to help readers internalize the command to trust and experience its transformative power in daily life.

## 4.4.1 Guided Prayer: Surrendering to Divine Wisdom

Begin your prayer with a moment of quiet reflection. Find a comfortable position and close your eyes. Breathe slowly, centering your thoughts on the promise that God's wisdom is greater than our own understanding.

Prayer:

"Gracious and Loving God, I come before You with an open heart, yearning to trust You fully. I confess that I often lean on my own understanding and allow fear and uncertainty to take hold. Today, I choose to surrender my doubts and place complete confidence in Your divine wisdom. Teach me to trust in You with all my heart, to acknowledge Your presence in every decision, and to follow Your guiding light without hesitation. May Your truth fill me with courage and peace. In Your holy name, I pray. Amen."

Allow the words to sink into your spirit. Reflect on the idea that trusting God is a continual choice—a daily decision to let go of control and embrace His providence.

## 4.4.2 Meditation on Proverbs 3:5-6

Meditation deepens our understanding by allowing the words of Scripture to resonate within us. Sit quietly with Proverbs 3:5-6 and let these verses permeate your inner life.

Meditative Reading:

Slowly read the passage:

- "Trust in the LORD with all your heart, and lean not on your own understanding."

- "In all your ways acknowledge Him, and He shall direct your paths."

Pause on each phrase. Imagine the weight of trust lifting from your shoulders as you commit your heart to God. Visualize your life as a path being illuminated by divine light—a path where every step is guided by His steady hand.

As you meditate, ask yourself:

- In what areas of my life do I most struggle to trust God fully?

- How can I acknowledge His presence in both the big decisions and the small everyday moments?

- What practical steps can I take today to replace self-reliance with confidence in His guidance?

Write down any thoughts, feelings, or insights that arise. Allow the meditation to become a conversation with God about your needs and aspirations.

## 4.4.3 Reflective Journaling: Trust in Action

Journaling is a powerful tool to internalize spiritual truths. Reflect on a recent time when trusting God transformed a challenging situation. Consider the following prompts:

- Describe an instance where you experienced uncertainty. How did you respond?

- In what ways did you see evidence of God's guidance during that time?

- What did you learn about yourself and about God from that experience?

- How can you cultivate more trust in similar circumstances moving forward?

Spend at least 10–15 minutes writing your reflections. Over time, revisit these entries to notice patterns of growth and moments where divine favor was clearly present in your life.

## 4.4.4 Affirmations for Daily Trust

Incorporate daily affirmations into your routine to solidify the internalization of trust in God. Begin your morning by affirming these words:

- "I trust in the LORD with all my heart."

- "I choose to acknowledge God's presence in every moment of my day."

- "I release my own limitations and embrace divine guidance."

- "Through faith and obedience, God directs my paths."

Repeat these affirmations as you go about your day, especially during moments of stress or decision-making. Let them serve as reminders that trust in the Lord is your constant source of strength.

## 4.4.5 Group Reflection and Prayer

For those who belong to a community of faith, consider gathering for group reflection. Share stories of personal experiences with trust and discuss how the promise of divine favor has shaped each individual's life. Corporate prayer and reflection not only build community but also reinforce the collective commitment to living out the biblical call to trust. Encourage group members to share strategies they have found effective in deepening their trust in God, thereby creating a supportive network where faith can flourish.

# 4.5 The Transformative Promise of Divine Favor

At its core, the call to trust in God carries the transformative promise of divine favor—a promise that transcends earthly limitations and opens the door to a richer, more meaningful life. By embracing trust, we align our hearts with the eternal truth that God's wisdom surpasses our own. This alignment brings forth:

- Clarity in Decision-Making: Trust clears away the murkiness of self-doubt and illuminates the path ahead.

- Resilience in Trials: When trials beset us, unwavering trust transforms hardship into opportunities for spiritual growth.

- A Deepened Relationship with God: As trust deepens into a lived experience, our relationship with God becomes more intimate, marked by genuine dependency and heartfelt communion.

- Manifestation of Blessings: The promise that "He shall direct your paths" is a continual assurance that living in trust brings tangible blessings—be it through emotional, spiritual, or even physical well-being.

The experience of divine favor is not measured by external markers alone but by the internal transformation that trust cultivates. As the believer learns to lean fully on God, the heart is remolded, priorities shift, and life takes on a purpose that reflects the gracious nature of its Creator.

# 4.6 Concluding Reflections

The call to trust in God, as revealed in Proverbs 3 and echoed throughout Scripture, is a foundational invitation to partake in a relationship that is both profound and practical. It is a call that asks us to relinquish our finite control and to embrace a faith that is as active as it is sincere. Trust, when combined with obedience and nurtured through daily devotional practices, provides a stable anchor amid life's uncertainties.

As you reflect on this chapter, consider how the key verses resonate with your own experience. How might the promises of divine favor encourage you to take bold steps of faith in your personal journey? In a world that often values self-reliance and personal achievement, the call to trust invites us to reorient our lives around the timeless truth of God's providence.

May the guided prayers, reflective meditations, and affirmations provided here serve as practical tools to help you internalize this call. Remember that the journey toward deepening trust is ongoing and that every moment—whether marked by joy or trial—is an opportunity to draw closer to God. As you continue to cultivate this trust, you will find that it transforms not only your perspective but also your actions, allowing you to live a life that truly reflects the enduring promise of divine favor.

In summary, the call to trust in God is not a passive suggestion but a vibrant, transformative invitation to live fully in the light of divine truth. By embracing the key verses, understanding the interplay of faith and obedience, and engaging in regular reflective practices, you become an active participant in the unfolding story of God's grace in the world. May your journey be filled with the assurance that as you trust in the Lord with all your heart, He will indeed direct your paths and shower you with His boundless favor.

Through this comprehensive exploration of trust as both a command and a promise, we have seen that to trust in God is to step into a dynamic relationship characterized by reliance, obedience, and perpetual growth. The call reverberates across time, urging each believer to experience the profound blessings that flow from surrendering fully to the divine will. Let this chapter guide your personal journey toward a deeper, more resilient trust—a trust that ultimately reshapes every facet of your life in accordance with God's eternal plan.

# Chapter 5: Embracing Wisdom's Guidance

In every age, wisdom has been portrayed as the guiding force that leads individuals toward moral clarity, ethical behavior, and a life of fulfillment. In the biblical tradition, wisdom is not merely an intellectual pursuit but a transformative influence—one that shapes character, directs choices, and ultimately leads to fruitfulness in every facet of life. This chapter explores the value of wisdom, outlines practical steps to acquire it as revealed in Proverbs 3, and offers personal applications through reflective questions and exercises designed to help you identify areas where wisdom is most needed in your life.

## The Value of Wisdom

### Wisdom as the Guiding Force for Moral and Ethical Living

Wisdom is depicted throughout Scripture and ancient literature as a beacon that illuminates the way through complex moral landscapes. It is more than a collection of clever sayings or moral maxims; it is a profound quality that roots a person's identity and actions in ethical principles and spiritual truths. In the biblical context, wisdom is shown to be a gift from God—a divine attribute that, when embraced, transforms human life.

1. Moral Compass:

Wisdom provides a moral compass in a world filled with competing values and shifting ethical standards. The teachings in Proverbs 3 remind us that true wisdom is measured not by worldly success but by the integrity of our actions. When a person acts wisely, choices are made with a clear vision of what is good, just, and pure. This kind of wisdom steers individuals away from self-centered pursuits and toward behaviors that honor community, justice, and compassion.

2. Ethical Living and Personal Integrity:

Wisdom intertwines with ethical living by nurturing personal integrity. It calls for a consistent adherence to values that create harmony in both private life and public affairs. A person who embodies wisdom is not swayed by short-term gains or the allure of popularity but stands firm on the principles of honesty, humility, and kindness. Biblical wisdom teaches that every choice, whether big or small, contributes to one's character and ultimately to one's destiny.

3. The Ripple Effect on Society:

Moreover, the value of wisdom extends beyond the individual—it is a communal treasure. When a community is led by wise principles, social relationships flourish, injustice is curtailed, and peace prevails. In Proverbs 3, the promise of divine favor for those who embrace wisdom highlights how ethical living, grounded in trust and righteousness, results in tangible benefits for society. A life marked by wisdom influences one's family, work, and community, generating a ripple effect that fosters collective well-being.

## The Transformative Impact of Embracing Wisdom

Embracing wisdom transforms how we experience life. It recalibrates our priorities, shifts our perspective from fleeting concerns to eternal truths, and helps us navigate adversity with resilience. Wisdom shows us that true fulfillment is found not in the accumulation of material wealth, but in a life aligned with divine purposes. The pursuit of wisdom encourages a continuous process of learning and self-improvement, where failures are seen as opportunities for growth and every experience contributes to a deeper understanding of life's mysteries.

# Practical Steps to Acquire Wisdom

## Understanding the Instructions in Proverbs 3

Proverbs 3 lays out a series of instructions that, when followed, lead to a fruitful and blessed life. These steps are practical and accessible, inviting readers to adopt a lifestyle that consistently reflects godly wisdom.

1. Trust in the Lord with All Your Heart:

The cornerstone instruction in Proverbs 3 is to "Trust in the LORD with all your heart and lean not on your own understanding" (Proverbs 3:5). This command encourages total reliance on God rather than on personal insight alone. The idea is to let go of self-sufficiency and acknowledge that true wisdom comes from divine guidance. Trusting in the Lord opens the door to His continuous direction and protection.

2. Acknowledge Him in All Your Ways:

The subsequent instruction, "In all your ways acknowledge Him, and He shall direct your paths" (Proverbs 3:6), complements this command. Acknowledgment implies a conscious decision to involve God in every decision, recognizing His supremacy in all aspects of life. This step is not just a verbal expression of faith; it is an active, constant orientation of one's actions and decisions toward divine principles.

3. Do Not Be Wise in Your Own Eyes:

Proverbs 3:7 advises against being "wise in your own eyes." This warns us against the pride that often accompanies self-assurance. Instead of relying solely on our human reasoning, which is limited and fallible, we must remain humble and open to God's greater wisdom. Humility is essential to be receptive to learning and receiving correction.

4. Honor the LORD with Your Wealth and Possessions:

The chapter also instructs believers to "Honor the LORD with your possessions, and with the first fruits of all your increase" (Proverbs 3:9). This act of honoring God with material blessings is a tangible expression of trust and gratitude. It represents a recognition that all that we have is ultimately a gift from God, and that sharing these blessings is a way to acknowledge His sovereignty and goodness.

5. Accept Divine Discipline as a Sign of Love:

Another key element in Proverbs 3 is understanding that divine discipline is a form of love. God disciplines those He loves, guiding them back to the right path when they stray. Rather than viewing discipline as punitive, it should be embraced as an opportunity for growth and refinement. Accepting this discipline is part of the process of acquiring wisdom—it means being teachable and recognizing that correction is a crucial ingredient in personal development.

6. Seek Wisdom, Understand, and Apply It:

The instructions in Proverbs 3 are not meant to be mere theoretical knowledge. They are practical steps that demand active engagement. This involves studying the Scriptures, reflecting on their meaning, and applying them in everyday contexts. The pursuit of wisdom is a lifelong journey of learning, where prayer, study, and community discussions play vital roles.

## Integrating Practical Wisdom into Daily Life

Acquiring wisdom is an iterative process involving daily choices and habits. Here are some actionable strategies based on the teachings of Proverbs 3:

- Daily Prayer and Meditation:

Begin and end each day with prayer, asking God to reveal His wisdom in every situation. Meditate on key verses and let them shape your day. Develop a routine that includes quiet moments of reflection to recalibrate your mind and spirit.

- Regular Study of Scripture:

Set aside dedicated time to read and study the Bible. Focus on passages that emphasize the importance of trust, humility, and obedience. Join a study group where the insights of Proverbs and other wisdom texts are discussed collectively.

- Practicing Generosity:

Honor God with your resources by practicing generosity. Whether it is through financial giving, volunteering, or sharing your time and talents, acts of kindness reflect a heart that recognizes the abundance of divine blessings.

- Embracing Humility and Learning:

Cultivate an attitude of humility by being open to feedback and correction. Recognize that wisdom often comes through life's challenges and that every experience can serve as a lesson. Reflect on your mistakes and consider how they can propel you toward a more enlightened future.

- Seeking Mentorship:

Identify mentors or role models who embody the qualities of wisdom. Learn from their experiences and let their guidance inspire you to walk the path of righteousness. Engage in conversations about how to integrate faith and practice in a meaningful way.

- Community Engagement:

Participate in community groups where discussions about faith and ethics are encouraged. The shared pursuit of wisdom can build strong relational bonds and create an environment where ethical living is both supported and celebrated.

# Personal Application: Reflection and Discussion

Translating the teachings of Proverbs 3 into everyday practices requires not only understanding but also self-reflection and active application.

Below are discussion questions and exercises designed to help you examine areas in your life where wisdom is needed and to develop strategies for embracing its guidance.

## Discussion Questions

1. Self-Reflection on Trust:

- In what ways do you struggle to trust in the Lord with your whole heart?

- Can you identify specific areas or decisions where you often rely on your own understanding rather than seeking divine guidance?

- How do these choices affect your overall well-being and relationships?

2. Understanding Humility:

- Reflect on a time when being "wise in your own eyes" led to a misstep or disappointment.

- What lessons did you learn from that experience about the importance of humility and seeking God's counsel?

3. Integration of Faith and Actions:

- How do you currently acknowledge God in your daily routines—at work, in your family interactions, or in times of solitude?

- What changes could you make to ensure that God's presence is more fully integrated into all aspects of your life?

4. The Role of Generosity and Discipline:

- Think about a moment when you experienced divine discipline. How did it influence your understanding of God's love and guidance?

- In what ways can you honor God with your resources in a tangible way that reflects both gratitude and trust?

# Reflective Exercises

## Exercise 1: Life Audit for Wisdom

- Objective: Identify areas in your life where wisdom is lacking or could be enhanced.
    - Instructions:
    1. Take a quiet moment and list out key aspects of your life (e.g., relationships, career, spiritual practices, health, financial management).
    2. Next to each area, rate your current level of reliance on personal judgment versus divine guidance on a scale of 1 to 10 (1 being complete self-reliance, 10 being full trust in God).
    3. Reflect on the areas where your score is lower. Consider practical ways you could shift toward greater reliance on God's wisdom—whether that means seeking counsel, praying more deliberately, or adopting new habits.

## Exercise 2: Daily Wisdom Journal

- Objective: Cultivate a habit of journaling as a means to reflect on and internalize the guidance of wisdom.
    - Instructions:
    1. Each day, write a short journal entry that begins with a key verse from Proverbs (e.g., Proverbs 3:5-6) and describe what that passage means to you today.
    2. Record instances during the day where you made decisions. Note moments when you trusted in your own understanding versus when you sought divine guidance.
    3. At the end of the week, review your entries to identify patterns and areas of growth, and set specific intentions for how you can deepen your reliance on wisdom in the coming week.

## Exercise 3: Guided Meditation Walk

- Objective: Experience wisdom in motion through a meditative walk that focuses on God's guidance.
    - Instructions:
    1. Choose a peaceful location where you can walk undisturbed for at least 20–30 minutes.
    2. As you begin your walk, silently recite a verse such as "In all your ways acknowledge Him" (Proverbs 3:6).
    3. With each step, focus on the idea that your path is being directed by a loving and wise guide. Reflect on the beauty around you as a reminder of the divine order.
    4. Conclude your walk by journaling any insights or thoughts that surfaced during your meditation.

## Exercise 4: Accountability Partnership

-Objective: Strengthen your commitment to embracing wisdom through shared accountability.
    - Instructions:
    1. Identify a trusted friend or mentor who shares your commitment to spiritual growth.
    2. Schedule a regular meeting—either weekly or biweekly—to discuss ways you have both been integrating the teachings of Proverbs into your lives.
    3. Share your challenges, celebrate your successes, and set mutual goals for areas where you both seek to deepen your trust in divine guidance.
    4. Document your discussions and review them periodically to see how your journey toward wisdom is evolving.

# Embracing Wisdom's Guidance: A Lifelong Journey

The pursuit of wisdom is not a one-time event, but a lifelong journey. It requires an ongoing commitment to learning, self-examination, and the willingness to adapt one's life in light of divine insights. As you embrace wisdom's guidance, you may discover that the challenges you once viewed as insurmountable become opportunities for growth and transformation. The promise of a fruitful life—characterized by moral clarity, ethical behavior, and spiritual fulfillment—is woven throughout the instructions in Proverbs 3.

True wisdom is both an inward and outward process. It begins in the heart, as you choose to trust beyond your limited understanding, and extends outward into every decision and interaction. The transformative power of wisdom is evident in how it reshapes priorities, heals broken relationships, and fosters a spirit of generosity and humility. By aligning your life with the principles laid out in Proverbs, you open yourself up to the possibility of experiencing profound blessings that impact not only you but also the people around you.

Remember that the journey to wisdom is iterative. There will be times of doubt, moments of failure, and challenges that test your resolve. In those moments, lean into the practices of prayer, reflection, and community. Allow yourself to be corrected and guided by the wisdom inherent in the Scriptures and the experiences of fellow believers. Over time, you will notice that the decisions you once struggled with become clearer, and the sense of peace that comes from trusting in divine guidance will become a constant presence in your life.

# Concluding Reflections

This chapter has explored the transformative role of wisdom as a guiding force for moral and ethical living. We have seen how the instructions in Proverbs 3 serve as a blueprint for acquiring wisdom—a process that begins with a steadfast trust in the Lord, requires humility, and is expressed through obedient, daily actions. Moreover, through reflective exercises and discussion questions, you are invited to actively engage with these teachings in a way that brings them into every aspect of your life.

Embracing wisdom's guidance means welcoming a lifestyle that prioritizes alignment with divine principles over transient, self-driven goals. It means recognizing that wisdom is not a destination, but a journey—one that continually challenges you to grow, learn, and evolve into the best version of yourself. As you take practical steps to integrate these teachings, you may find that the path to a fruitful life becomes illuminated with hope, purpose, and a deep sense of inner peace.

May this chapter serve not only as an intellectual exploration of wisdom but also as a practical guide that empowers you to live a life defined by ethical integrity, reflective decision-making, and a heart open to divine guidance. Embrace each day as an opportunity to further incorporate wisdom into your life, confident in the promise that as you do, you are walking in alignment with a higher purpose that brings lasting blessing and fulfillment.

# Chapter 6: The Paradox of Humility and Prosperity

The biblical text of Proverbs 3 presents a fascinating tension—a paradox—between humility and prosperity. On one level, humility is often associated with modesty, lowly status, and a willingness to submit, while prosperity is typically linked with achievement, success, and a certain self-assurance. Yet, in the ancient wisdom tradition as articulated in Proverbs 3, humility is not only a virtue for its own sake but also the very foundation upon which both spiritual wealth and material well-being are built. In this chapter, we will explore this paradox in depth. We begin with an examination of humility as a foundation for both personal growth and divine favor. Then, we move on to a detailed analysis of what Proverbs 3 teaches about wealth and success, paying particular attention to the promises that encompass physical, emotional, and spiritual well-being. Finally, we consider the modern implications of these ancient teachings, exploring how contemporary views on success and humility can be enriched—and even redefined—by returning to this wisdom.

## Humility as a Foundation

### The Biblical Perspective on Humility

Humility in the biblical tradition is far more than a mere self-effacement or a denial of one's talents. It is the recognition of one's position before God—a deep awareness that all wisdom, power, and prosperity ultimately come from a divine source. Proverbs 3 does not present humility as an outdated ideal or a concession to subjugation; rather, it is the necessary standpoint from which true prosperity is achieved. Humility is both the entry point and the continual posture of a life that is open to receiving divine grace.

In many biblical passages, humility is portrayed as the beginning of wisdom. Proverbs 11:2, for instance, notes that "When pride comes, then comes disgrace, but with humility comes wisdom." Here, humility is seen as a safeguard against the pitfalls of pride—a state of being that blinds one to one's true limitations. In our modern context, humility often seems counterintuitive in a society that prizes self-promotion and individual achievement. Yet, the ancient wisdom reminds us that true strength comes from acknowledging our interdependence with a power beyond ourselves and that our human limitations are precisely what make us receptive to God's infinite wisdom.

## Humility as a Pathway to Spiritual Wealth

Humility opens up the heart to spiritual riches. This is the wealth that transcends material measures—a wealth characterized by inner peace, clarity of purpose, and a deep connection with the divine. When one humbles oneself, the barriers erected by ego fall away, and one is free to receive insight and guidance. In this state of openness, the heart becomes fertile ground for love, compassion, and divine revelation. This spiritual wealth often serves as the wellspring for a greater understanding of life's deeper meaning.

Proverbs 3 highlights that those who trust in the Lord and practice humility are promised favor that extends beyond the spiritual realm. The text declares that trust is rewarded not just with eternal blessings, but with tangible benefits that influence everyday circumstances. The paradox is that it is the humble, who recognize their need for divine guidance, who are positioned to receive the fullness of God's blessings—a blessing that includes spiritual renewal as well as material prosperity.

## Humility and the Receptivity to Divine Discipline

Integral to the paradox of humility is the acceptance of divine discipline. The process of growth, as envisioned in Proverbs, is not one without correction. True humility acknowledges that errors and misjudgments will occur, and it embraces correction as an opportunity for growth rather than a personal attack. This receptivity to discipline is presented as a sign of maturity and wisdom. When one is humble, one does not resist the corrective whispers of divine love; instead, one receives them as necessary inputs for transformation.

This view stands in stark contrast to cultural narratives that equate discipline with failure. In the scriptural perspective, discipline is a manifestation of love—a guidepost that points the way back to the right path. It is in the humility of accepting correction that the potential for lasting transformation is realized.

# Wealth and Success in Proverbs 3

## The Promises of Material and Emotional Prosperity

Proverbs 3 offers a series of blessings that appear to address all dimensions of human flourishing. Perhaps the most well-known passage in the chapter promises that trusting in God will lead to prosperity, long life, and favor. Such promises include tangible benefits like health and material stability, as well as intangible rewards like emotional resilience and spiritual peace. This duality reflects the comprehensive vision of a well-lived life in the biblical worldview.

The blessings described in Proverbs 3 are not presented as an automatic guarantee for the pious; rather, they are contingent upon a heartfelt trust in God and a refusal to rely solely on one's own understanding. The metaphor of a path being "directed" by the Lord (Proverbs 3:6) implies a journey where each step is under divine supervision, ensuring that even when the terrain is rocky or treacherous, there is a secure way forward. It is this assurance that motivates many believers to adopt humility as a core value—the understanding that human intellect and might are insufficient without the guiding hand of God.

## Material Well-Being and the Ethics of Prosperity

Yet, within Proverbs 3, the notion of prosperity is not limited to material accumulation. In the biblical framework, material wealth is often intertwined with ethical conduct. Wealth, when granted by divine favor, is meant to be used for the welfare of the individual and the community. The admonition to "Honor the LORD with your possessions" (Proverbs 3:9) is a call not only to generosity but also to the recognition that wealth is a trust—a responsibility to steward resources in accordance with divine principles.

When one practices humility, one is more apt to see wealth as a tool for service rather than as an end in itself. This reorientation challenges the modern narrative of success, which often measures prosperity solely in terms of financial gain and personal status. Instead, the biblical account suggests that true wealth includes the love, generosity, and moral clarity that stem from a life centered on God. The convergence of humility with ethical use of wealth creates a dynamic where success is measured both by the quality of one's character and by the tangible benefits that flow from living in alignment with divine will.

## Emotional and Physical Well-Being: An Integrated Approach

The blessings of Proverbs 3 extend to physical and emotional realms. Trusting in the Lord is depicted as a remedy for the anxieties and stresses of life. Emotionally, those who rely on divine guidance experience a sense of peace that surpasses all understanding—a peace that stabilizes the inner self even amidst external turmoil. Physically, the promise of long life and health is both motivational and reassuring. The verse that speaks to the directorship of one's path implies that the wisdom of God is a safeguard, protecting and sustaining the individual through the inevitable hardships of life.

This integrated approach to well-being highlights that prosperity in Proverbs 3 is comprehensive. It is not compartmentalized into separate domains; rather, it reflects a holistic vision of flourishing. Humility, therefore, is the cornerstone of this integrated model: by acknowledging one's limitations and seeking divine counsel, a person becomes open to a cascade of blessings that enrich every aspect of life.

# Modern Implications: Re-examining Success and Humility

## Contemporary Views on Success

In today's society, success is frequently measured by external markers such as wealth, status, and personal achievement. Media, corporate culture, and even educational institutions often celebrate a particular kind of self-assured ambition that prizes self-reliance above all else. The modern narrative can, at times, be at odds with the ancient wisdom that elevates humility as the source of true strength and prosperity.

Contemporary success frequently valorizes assertiveness and the relentless pursuit of personal goals—a model that may encourage self-centeredness and an overemphasis on individual accomplishment. In such a context, admitting one's need for guidance, especially from a transcendent source, may be viewed as a weakness. Yet, if we pause to consider the biblical message, we see that the wisdom of Proverbs 3 offers an alternative paradigm: one where humility is not a sign of defeat but an expression of deep, inner strength.

## The Paradox Revisited in Modern Life

The paradox of humility and prosperity challenges modern sensibilities in profound ways. Far from being antithetical to success, genuine humility can be the catalyst for sustainable, authentic achievement. Consider the idea that in a rapidly changing and often unpredictable world, the ability to remain flexible and open—to recognize that one does not have all the answers—is in fact one of the greatest strengths a person can possess. Humility encourages learning, fosters collaborative relationships, and allows for innovation by recognizing that every individual has limitations.

For modern leaders, whether in business, politics, or community organizations, humility is increasingly recognized as a critical component of effective leadership. Leaders who are humble are better at listening, more resilient in the face of failures, and more capable of inspiring loyalty and trust among their teams. The biblical invitation to "not be wise in your own eyes" resonates deeply in an era marked by overconfidence and hubris. By relinquishing the need to control every outcome, modern individuals and leaders can create environments where collective wisdom flourishes.

## Reconciling Material Prosperity with Ethical Living

In today's world, material success is often achieved at the expense of ethical considerations. Greed, exploitation, and a narrow focus on profit have marred many spheres of economic and social life. The wisdom of Proverbs 3, however, offers a counter-narrative: one in which material prosperity is both a blessing and a responsibility. True prosperity, as framed by biblical teachings, is integrally connected to ethical living. Wealth is not an end in itself but a means to achieve a higher purpose—one that benefits not only the individual but also society at large.

Modern consumers and investors are increasingly aware of this, gravitating toward ethical businesses and socially responsible investments. The revival of interest in corporate social responsibility and conscious capitalism reflects an emerging consensus that success and integrity need not be mutually exclusive. By embracing humility and redefining prosperity through the lens of wisdom, modern society can work toward a model of success that incorporates fairness, generosity, and a deep respect for human dignity.

## Relevance for Personal Growth and Community Flourishing

On a personal level, the paradox of humility and prosperity has the power to transform everyday life. It challenges individuals to reflect on what constitutes true success and to reexamine the values that guide their decisions. In a culture saturated with images of unattainable wealth and superficial triumph, the humble pursuit of wisdom offers a refreshing counterpoint—a model of living that prioritizes inner growth, relationships, and spiritual well-being over transient accolades.

Community life, too, stands to benefit from embracing the wisdom of humility. Societies built on the principles of care, collaboration, and mutual respect tend to be more resilient and cohesive. When individuals within a community adopt a posture of humility, they become more receptive to the needs of others, willing to share resources, and more inclined to support collective initiatives that promote common good. In this way, the ancient wisdom of Proverbs 3 can serve as a foundation not only for personal prosperity but also for thriving, ethically grounded communities.

## Synthesis: Integrating Humility and Prosperity in a Modern Context

The paradox of humility and prosperity as presented in Proverbs 3 is not an outdated relic of antiquity—it is a living challenge and invitation for each generation. At its core, this wisdom teaches that prosperity is not merely the accumulation of wealth or status; it is the fruit of a humble, obedient heart that is open to divine guidance. Humility, far from being a mark of weakness, is the dynamic foundation upon which all true blessings are built. It facilitates growth, enhances leadership, and creates fertile ground for both spiritual and material well-being.

In a modern context, this integrated vision is both radical and revitalizing. It calls into question the dominant narratives that equate success with ego, competition, and self-reliance. Instead, it presents an alternative paradigm—a model of success measured by generosity, ethical conduct, and the capacity to listen and learn. This model challenges individuals and communities to reassess their priorities, encouraging practices that nurture both personal fulfillment and social responsibility.

For the individual seeker, the path laid out in Proverbs 3 is a journey of continual transformation. It involves daily choices: choosing to trust rather than to control, to be humble rather than self-aggrandizing, and to use one's blessings in service of others. These choices, though sometimes countercultural, pave the way for a holistic kind of prosperity that integrates physical, emotional, and spiritual dimensions.

For those in leadership, the message of humility is a reminder that true influence comes from a willingness to be vulnerable, to share credit, and to lift others up. Leaders who exemplify humility create environments where collaborative decision-making thrives and where ethical practices are the norm rather than the exception. Such an approach to leadership not only increases organizational resilience but also fosters a culture of trust and mutual respect.

# Concluding Reflections

The paradox of humility and prosperity presented in Proverbs 3 invites us to reimagine what it means to succeed. In the ancient wisdom, humility is not just a moral ideal but the very foundation of a rich, fulfilling life. It is the key that unlocks both spiritual wealth and material well-being, bridging the gap between the sacred and the everyday. By embracing humility, we open ourselves to divine blessings that transform our relationships, guide our decisions, and shape our communities.

As you reflect on the teachings of this chapter, consider the ways in which humility has played a role in your own life. Ask yourself: Are there areas where self-reliance has hindered your progress? How might a greater openness to guidance—both divine and communal—lead to more holistic prosperity? Let these questions inspire personal introspection and a renewed commitment to living a life in harmony with the wisdom of Proverbs.

In our modern age, where the definitions of success are often narrow and self-centered, the call to embrace humility offers a liberating alternative. It challenges us to redefine prosperity so that it encompasses not only financial stability and status but also the richness of character, the depth of relationships, and the vibrancy of spiritual life. In doing so, we align ourselves with a tradition that has guided countless generations toward lives of lasting impact and fulfillment.

May the insights of this chapter encourage you to adopt a posture of humble dependence on divine wisdom, to pursue success that honors ethical and spiritual dimensions, and to contribute to a community where every blessing is shared. In embracing the paradox of humility and prosperity, we find that true wealth flows not from what we accumulate for ourselves but from how we live in service to others and in faithful trust of the One who directs our paths.

Let this integrated approach be your guide as you move forward—confident that by remaining humble, you invite an abundance of blessings that enrich every aspect of your life, both now and for generations to come.

# Chapter 7: The Role of Discipline and Correction

Discipline and correction are sometimes viewed in modern society as punitive or negative experiences. However, in the biblical tradition, particularly within the wisdom literature of Proverbs, discipline is redefined as an expression of divine love and care—a necessary element for growth, maturity, and a righteous life. In this chapter, we explore the transformative role of divine discipline, examine how personal growth is intimately tied to accepting correction and learning from life's challenges, and provide practical strategies along with reflective questions for incorporating discipline and correction into our daily lives.

## 7.1 Understanding Divine Discipline

### The Biblical Perspective on Discipline

From a biblical standpoint, discipline is far more than a system of punishment; it is a manifestation of God's love. Numerous passages in the Bible, especially within the wisdom literature, illustrate how God's corrections are intended to guide, refine, and restore rather than to condemn. For example, in Proverbs 3:11-12 it is written:

"My son, do not despise the LORD's discipline, and do not resent his rebuke, because the LORD disciplines those he loves, as a father the son he delights in."

This passage encapsulates the key message that discipline is a reflection of God's deep care. In the same way that a loving parent corrects a child out of concern for their wellbeing, divine discipline is intended to help believers grow into their true selves. It is an invitation to a deeper, more honest relationship with God—a relationship that is predicated on trust, humility, and the recognition that correction is a means of protection and progress.

## Divine Discipline: Love and Care in Action

Divine discipline is not arbitrary or harsh; it is methodical and purposeful. When the Scriptures describe discipline as an expression of God's love, they remind us that correction is woven into the fabric of a caring relationship. Several key themes emerge from the biblical view on discipline:

1. Restorative, Not Retributive:

Divine discipline aims to restore rather than to simply punish. It is designed to help individuals correct their course so that they may enjoy the full blessings that God intends. The underlying purpose is always redemptive—guiding a person back to the path of righteousness.

2. A Sign of Parental Concern:

Just as a parent disciplines a child out of genuine concern for the child's welfare, divine correction is an indicator of God's active interest in the spiritual development of His people. When believers face adversity or correction, it is a tangible reminder that they are cherished and that God desires to see them flourish.

3. Preparation for Greater Responsibility:

Discipline prepares believers for the challenges of life. It instills virtues such as patience, resilience, and self-control—qualities that are essential for personal growth and for living a life that reflects divine wisdom. Through the experience of correction, individuals learn to harness their strengths and navigate their weaknesses.

4. A Catalyst for Humility:

Recognizing and accepting correction requires humility—a willingness to acknowledge that one's understanding is limited and that there is always room for growth. This humility is a virtue celebrated in the Bible because it opens the door to genuine wisdom and transformation.

## Scriptural Examples of Divine Discipline

Throughout the Bible, there are numerous examples where God's discipline leads to a greater good. The narrative of King David, for instance, reveals a man who, despite his significant failures, experienced God's corrective discipline and emerged with a deeper understanding of his dependence on divine guidance. Similarly, the apostle Paul frequently referred to his own experiences of hardship and correction as means by which God molded him into an effective vessel of His message. These examples underscore that while discipline may be challenging in the moment, it ultimately bears fruit in the form of growth, learning, and renewed purpose.

# 7.2 Learning from Correction: A Pathway to Personal Growth

## The Necessity of Correction in the Journey of Faith

Personal growth is rarely achieved without encountering challenges, setbacks, or the discomfort of being corrected. In fact, the journey toward maturity is marked by moments when our limited perspectives are expanded through constructive correction. The Bible teaches that no one is exempt from the need for discipline; rather, it is a universal experience among those who seek to live in accordance with God's principles.

When we acknowledge that correction is an inherent part of our spiritual and personal evolution, we begin to view our mistakes and failures not as final verdicts of inadequacy but as opportunities to learn and refine our character. This shift in perspective is transformative—it allows us to move beyond pride and defensiveness into a posture of openness, where we actively seek and learn from the guidance provided to us.

## The Process of Learning and Transformation

1. Recognition of Error:

The first step in learning from correction is the honest recognition that our behavior or understanding may be flawed. This is not an admission of defeat but an acceptance of human fallibility. Recognizing our mistakes opens the pathway to growth.

2. Reflection on the Correction:

After acknowledging an error, it is vital to reflect on the nature of the correction. What lesson is being imparted? How does this correction align with the broader principles of divine wisdom? Reflection often involves prayer, meditation, or even discussions with trusted mentors, allowing us to internalize the correction and understand its implications.

3. Repentance and Commitment to Change:

True learning from correction involves not only understanding the mistake but also making a conscious commitment to change. Repentance here is not about self-condemnation; rather, it is a proactive decision to realign one's actions with divine guidance. As the Scriptures advise, "correct your ways, and you will be healed" (Proverbs 4:27, interpreted within the broader context of wisdom literature).

4. Integration and Continuous Improvement:

The lessons gleaned from correction are best put into practice by integrating them into daily life. Continuous improvement is an ongoing process, where every correction is seen as a stepping stone towards becoming a wiser, more resilient individual. Over time, these efforts culminate in a life that is marked by balance, humility, and a deep reliance on divine grace.

## The Role of Life's Challenges

Life's challenges, by their very nature, are opportunities disguised as difficulties. The moments of trial and error, when encountered with an open heart, have the potential to be profound teachers. When we face adversity, we are often forced to reevaluate our methods, reconsider our priorities, and ultimately, to grow in character. The lens through which we view these challenges is critical: rather than seeing them as pure misfortune, we can understand them as divine interventions designed to steer us toward a more authentic and purpose-driven life.

## Personal Testimonies of Transformation

History and personal testimonies provide countless accounts of how embracing correction has led to breakthrough moments. Whether in the stories of biblical figures or modern-day narratives, the common thread is the transformative power of accepting discipline. Individuals who have experienced the turning point of divine correction often report not only improved decision-making but a renewed sense of inner peace and clarity about their life's purpose. These stories remind us that while the process of being corrected can be painful, it is ultimately a gift—a necessary mechanism for cultivating wisdom and resilience.

# 7.3 Application in Daily Life

Integrating discipline and correction into daily life involves shifting our perceptions and habits. It requires us to be proactive in seeking growth, to be receptive to feedback, and to transform challenges into opportunities for self-improvement. Below are several practical strategies and reflective questions designed to help you embrace discipline as a positive force in your everyday experience.

## Practical Tips for Embracing Discipline and Correction

1. Cultivate a Heart of Humility:

Begin by acknowledging that no matter how knowledgeable or skilled we may become, there is always room for growth. Humility is the foundation upon which the ability to accept correction rests. Consider starting each day with a moment of prayer or meditation dedicated to surrendering your ego and asking for openness to learn.

2. Establish Regular Self-Reflection Practices:

Set aside time on a daily or weekly basis to review your actions, decisions, and attitudes. Journaling can be particularly useful in this regard. Reflect on moments when you resisted advice or when a setback taught you an unexpected lesson. Ask yourself, "What can I learn from this experience?" and "How might this correction guide me toward better choices in the future?"

3. Seek Constructive Feedback:

Embrace opportunities for feedback from trusted friends, mentors, or colleagues. Rather than viewing criticism as a threat, reframe it as a source of valuable insight. Ask for specific suggestions on how you might improve, and listen with an open mind. Remember, constructive feedback is an external reflection of God's corrective love manifested through others in your community.

4. Develop a Growth Mindset:

Adopt the perspective that mistakes are merely stepping stones on the path of continuous improvement. Celebrate your efforts to learn from missteps, and view challenges as opportunities to strengthen your character. Remind yourself that every correction is a part of the journey toward becoming a more wise, compassionate, and effective individual.

5. Create an Accountability Network:

Surround yourself with a community that values growth, humility, and integrity. Whether it's a small group at your place of worship, a study group, or a peer mentoring system, an accountability network can provide support during times of correction and celebrate your progress during moments of success.

6. Practice Gratitude for Correction:

Whenever you receive constructive criticism or experience setbacks, practice gratitude. Acknowledge that these moments, though uncomfortable, are gifts that drive you to a higher purpose. Express thanks for the opportunity to refine your character and for the guidance that helps you realign with your true path.

## Reflective Questions for Personal Examination

To deepen your understanding and facilitate internal change, consider the following reflective questions:

- Self-Awareness and Humility:

- In which areas of my life do I find it most difficult to accept correction?

- How does pride manifest in my decisions, and what steps can I take to cultivate a more humble attitude?

- Understanding Correction:

- Can I recall a recent incident where correction led to a positive change in my life? What did I learn from that experience?

- How do I typically react to constructive feedback, and how might I adjust my response to view it as an opportunity for growth?

- Integration into Daily Living:

- What daily routines or habits can I modify or establish to make space for regular reflection and self-improvement?

- How can I incorporate prayer or meditation into my schedule as a way of seeking divine guidance in my responses to correction?

- Community and Accountability:

- Who in my community can serve as a mentor or accountability partner to help me embrace discipline more fully?

- In what ways can I contribute to creating a culture of constructive feedback and mutual growth within my family, workplace, or community?

## Practical Exercise: The Daily Correction Journal

One effective method to internalize discipline and correction is to maintain a "Daily Correction Journal." Here's a step-by-step guide for this exercise:

1. Set Aside Time Each Day:

Dedicate at least 10–15 minutes at the end of each day for reflection.

2. Record Moments of Correction:

Write down any incidents, comments, or personal insights that functioned as corrective feedback. This could be a critique you received at work, a moment of self-realization about a recurring habit, or an unexpected lesson from a challenging situation.

3. Reflect on the Lessons Learned:

For each entry, note what lesson you took away. Ask yourself, "How does this correction help me align more closely with my values and spiritual goals?"

4. Plan for Future Improvement:

Write down a concrete action plan for how you will integrate the lesson learned into your behavior tomorrow. This might include a small change in routine, a new approach to problem-solving, or a commitment to seek further feedback on a particular area.

5. Review and Reflect Weekly:

At the end of the week, review your journal entries. Look for recurring themes or patterns that indicate areas where you can focus your growth efforts. Celebrate the progress you have made and set new goals for the following week.

## Practical Exercise: Building an Accountability Circle

Another valuable practice is forming or joining an accountability circle. This group can offer both encouragement and gentle, loving correction. Here is how to get started:

1. Identify Trusted Individuals:

Select a few people who share your commitment to personal growth and who are capable of providing honest and constructive feedback.

2. Establish a Regular Meeting Time:

Set a consistent schedule—weekly, biweekly, or monthly—where you can gather to discuss challenges and progress.

3. Set Clear Guidelines:

Agree on some basic principles for your meetings, such as confidentiality, respect, and a focus on growth rather than criticism for its own sake.

4. Share Personal Reflections:

During meetings, take turns sharing insights from your Daily Correction Journals, discussing lessons learned, and outlining your plans for improvement.

5. Offer Mutual Support:

Use the meetings to offer encouragement and practical advice. Sometimes hearing a different perspective can illuminate aspects of your own behavior that you might not have seen.

## 7.4 Embracing Correction as a Path to Empowerment

Ultimately, the role of discipline and correction in the journey of life is one of empowerment. Embracing correction helps us transcend our limitations and cultivate the resilience needed to navigate life's unpredictable challenges. It is through disciplined self-examination and the willingness to accept guidance that we become more fully realized individuals—capable of true transformation and equipped to make a positive impact on the world around us.

When we reframe correction as an act of divine love rather than as personal failure, we free ourselves from the fear of making mistakes. This freedom is essential for creativity, risk-taking, and genuine progress. It allows us to step boldly into our futures, confident that every corrective experience is a stepping stone leading toward a more fulfilling and purpose-driven life.

# 7.5 Concluding Reflections

The biblical wisdom of Proverbs teaches that discipline is far from punitive—it is a vital expression of divine care that shapes us into wiser, more compassionate, and ultimately more successful individuals. Accepting correction and learning from our challenges are essential ingredients in the recipe for personal growth. Through humility and a willingness to be shaped by the corrective love of God, we build a foundation that supports both our spiritual journey and our day-to-day lives.

In embracing discipline, we learn that life's setbacks are not roadblocks but rather signposts directing us toward a better way of living. We discover that our errors and missteps, when viewed through the lens of divine love, become opportunities for profound transformation. By integrating daily practices such as self-reflection, journaling, meditation, and accountability, we position ourselves to continually learn and evolve.

As you move forward from this chapter, ask yourself how you can adopt these practices in your daily routine. How might the lessons of divine discipline transform the way you face challenges? In what ways can you become more receptive to the loving corrections that guide you toward your true potential? May these reflections and practical strategies inspire you to welcome discipline into your life as an invaluable tool for growth, empowerment, and deeper alignment with God's enduring wisdom.

By viewing every corrective experience as an opportunity to improve, you join a timeless tradition of those who understand that true strength lies in humility, that transformation is fueled by a willingness to learn, and that the road to lasting success is paved with both discipline and grace. Embrace this journey, knowing that each step toward accepting correction is a step toward a richer, more purposeful life.

# Chapter 8: The Spiritual Transformation Through Wisdom

Wisdom, as depicted in the biblical tradition, is far more than a collection of rules or a repository of clever sayings. It is a dynamic, transformative force that reshapes our inner lives, renews our spirit, and guides us toward a higher understanding of ourselves and our relationship with the divine. Proverbs 3 not only provides practical guidance but also paints a portrait of a life reimagined—a life where the union of heart and mind, nurtured through humility and trust, leads to genuine spiritual transformation. In this chapter, we explore the themes of transformation that result from the pursuit and embrace of biblical wisdom. We examine the renewal of the heart and mind as integral to developing character, and we consider historical and modern testimonies of individuals who have experienced profound change by incorporating the principles of divine wisdom into their lives.

## Transformation Themes: The Pathway to Inner Renewal

### Wisdom as a Catalyst for Transformation

Acquiring wisdom, particularly as it is laid out in Proverbs, initiates a process of inner transformation—a turning of the heart and renewal of the mind that affects every aspect of life. At its core, wisdom is about perceiving truth, discerning what is good, and aligning our lives with what is right and just. This shift in perspective is transformative because it moves us from self-reliance and limited human understanding to a posture of open dependency on divine guidance.

The process of transformation begins with a sincere realization that our own ways of understanding and living are flawed. The call of Proverbs 3:5—"Trust in the LORD with all your heart, and lean not on your own understanding"—is an invitation to abandon ego and pride. It is a call to let go of the false security we find in our limited logic and to embrace a broader, more compassionate perspective. This insight can spark a fundamental change in how we relate to the world around us.

## Inner Transformation and a Renewed Spirit

When one accepts wisdom, the process of inner transformation follows. This journey is characterized by several key changes:

1. A Change in Priorities:

With wisdom comes the realization that what truly matters is not the fleeting success measured by worldly standards but the enduring values of integrity, compassion, and spiritual maturity. The transformation is marked by a realignment of goals—one where personal ambitions give way to a pursuit of lasting peace and moral clarity. This shift often results in diminished selfish desires and a heightened concern for the welfare of others.

2. The Cultivation of Humility:

A humble heart is the fertile ground on which wisdom blossoms. As individuals begin to recognize their limitations, they become open to correction and guidance. Humility transforms character by enabling a person to learn continuously, to value the contributions of others, and to accept that true knowledge comes from a source greater than one's own mind. It is the acknowledgement of human frailty that opens the door to divine strength.

3. Renewal of the Spirit:

Transformation through wisdom renews the spirit in a way that infuses life with purpose and direction. When wisdom is internalized, it acts as a wellspring that revitalizes one's inner being. This renewal is experienced as a profound sense of peace that endures despite external circumstances. It is a spiritual awakening—a rising above the routine and often chaotic demands of daily life that reconnects the individual with a more transcendent reality.

4. Enhanced Discernment and Moral Clarity:

Wisdom sharpens our ability to discern right from wrong. With a transformed mind, the decisions we make are filtered through the lens of ethical awareness. This moral clarity brings consistency in our actions, fortifying our character and providing a steady foundation on which to base all of our relationships and choices.

## The Journey as Lifelong Transformation

Importantly, the transformation resulting from embracing wisdom is not a one-time event. Instead, it is a continual process—a lifelong journey of growth, learning, and self-renewal. Each encounter with divine insight, each moment of self-reflection, reinforces a cycle of transformation. In this way, wisdom creates an ongoing evolution of the self, where every day offers new opportunities to reflect, adapt, and progress toward a more enlightened state of being.

# Heart and Mind Renewal: The Interplay That Shapes Character

## The Dual Renewal: Where Emotion Meets Intellect

The transformation described in Proverbs 3 is not solely an intellectual exercise—it engages both the heart and the mind. The biblical view of wisdom insists that true understanding involves an integration of emotion and reason. The heart, seen as the seat of desire, passion, and moral sensitivity, works in concert with the mind, which processes logic, knowledge, and discernment. This dual renewal is essential for a balanced transformation.

When a person's heart is renewed, they experience a shift in emotional energy. Negative traits such as fear, anger, or pride give way to love, humility, and compassion. The mind, freed from the chains of cynical self-reliance, starts to appreciate the broader truths of life. This is precisely what Proverbs 3 illustrates: a life reoriented away from arrogance and towards a deep, abiding trust in a higher authority. A renewed heart inspires acts of kindness and empathy, while a renewed mind sharpens one's capacity to make wise, ethical decisions.

## The Interconnectedness of Heart and Mind

Several themes in Proverbs 3 highlight the inseparability of heart and mind. Consider the imperative to "Trust in the LORD with all your heart." Trust, although often considered an emotional state, calls for a decision that involves both heart and mind. It is not merely an automatic response but a deliberate act of faith—a choice to believe in God's inherent goodness and to apply that trust in every situation.

This interplay is at the core of character transformation. The heart, when aligned with the divine, becomes receptive to compassion and sacrifice. Meanwhile, the mind, sharpened by the pursuit of wisdom, discerns the ethical implications of every decision. Together, they form a powerful synergy: the heart motivates, and the mind directs. As a person grows in wisdom, this symbiosis ensures that decisions are not only rationally sound but also emotionally resonant and spiritually uplifting.

## Transforming Character Through Renewal

A transformed heart and mind manifest in an evolved character. Key virtues such as perseverance, integrity, and courage are cultivated through ongoing reflection and application of divine wisdom. When individuals allow their hearts to be softened by love and their minds to be enlightened by truth, they become more resilient in the face of adversity. This transformation is seen in a gentler, more graceful response to life's challenges, characterized by an unwavering sense of purpose and a balanced perspective on success and failure.

Moreover, as the heart and mind align with divine truth, individuals begin to exhibit fruits that benefit not only themselves but also the communities in which they live. This transformation leads to better interpersonal relationships, greater empathy, and a more profound sense of justice. In essence, the renewal of heart and mind is the engine behind a transformed character, one that inspires others to seek wisdom and live in a manner that reflects the highest ideals.

# Testimonies and Case Studies: Real-Life Transformations Through Biblical Wisdom

## Historical Examples of Transformation

Throughout history, there have been countless examples of individuals whose lives were radically transformed through the embrace of biblical wisdom. One of the most notable examples is the life of Saint Augustine. Augustine's early life was fraught with moral confusion and inner turmoil. However, upon encountering the works of the Church Fathers and the stirring truths of Scripture, he experienced a profound internal conversion. His subsequent writings, particularly in his seminal work *Confessions*, document his journey from a life marked by arrogance and indulgence to one of deep humility and faith—a journey catalyzed by the transformative power of wisdom.

Similarly, the life of John Wesley, the founder of the Methodist movement, is another powerful testimony. Wesley's transformation was marked by a sincere reliance on God's grace and a humble commitment to living out the teachings of Scripture. Through his emphasis on personal holiness, scriptural reflection, and a community-oriented approach to faith, Wesley redefined success for countless believers—shifting the focus from worldly wealth to spiritual prosperity.

## Modern-Day Testimonies of Transformation

In addition to historical figures, contemporary accounts offer compelling evidence of the transformative power of biblical wisdom. Consider the testimony of Linda, a business executive who faced overwhelming stress and moral dilemmas in a cutthroat corporate environment. Despite her outward success, Linda felt spiritually bankrupt. After encountering the teachings of Proverbs during a period of personal crisis, she began to reassess her life. Embracing the principles of trust, humility, and ethical living, Linda gradually reoriented her priorities. Over time, she reported experiencing not only improved mental clarity and emotional resilience but also a surprising shift in her business practices—a move away from ruthless competitiveness toward a leadership style characterized by empathy, fairness, and collaboration. Linda's story illustrates how wisdom can facilitate a radical inner transformation that bears fruit both personally and professionally.

Another modern example comes from David, a former athlete who struggled with the pressures of professional sports and the disillusionment that followed a career-ending injury. Feeling lost and without purpose, David turned to a local ministry that emphasized the wisdom of Scripture. Through dedicated study, prayer, and mentorship, David learned to reframe his sense of identity—not as a fallen star defined by his athletic achievements, but as a beloved child of God with talents that could be redeployed in service to others. Today, David leads community programs that empower others who have faced adversity, using his own journey as a beacon of hope. His transformation underscores a recurring theme in Proverbs: that wisdom not only restores hope but also equips individuals to effect positive change in the world around them.

## Lessons from Testimonies: Insights for Personal Transformation

These testimonies, both historical and modern, offer valuable lessons for anyone seeking spiritual transformation through wisdom:

1. The Importance of a Changed Perspective:

Transformation begins with the recognition that our current way of life may be misaligned with our highest values. Whether in the throes of personal failure or during moments of spiritual clarity, the impetus to change often comes from experiencing the gap between what is and what could be. Biblical wisdom provides a roadmap for bridging that gap.

2. Resilience Through Embracing Correction:

Both historical and modern accounts highlight the role of correction and discipline in fostering growth. Instead of resisting difficult lessons, transformed individuals embrace them as opportunities to learn and develop resilience. This mindset is essential for cultivating lasting change.

3. The Synergy of Community and Mentorship:

Many personal transformations documented in these testimonies were not accomplished in isolation. The guidance of mentors, the support of communities, and the accountability provided by like-minded individuals all contributed to deeper spiritual renewal. Engaging with a community that values wisdom can accelerate one's own transformation.

4. Integration of Inner Renewal into Every Aspect of Life:

True transformation is holistic, affecting not only our inner lives but also how we interact with the world. Whether in our personal relationships, professional endeavors, or community engagements, the principles of biblical wisdom—trust, humility, and ethical living—serve as a compass that directs our actions and enriches our experiences.

# Practical Steps Towards Spiritual Transformation Through Wisdom

Transformation is a journey that requires deliberate action. Based on the insights and testimonies above, here are some practical steps you can take to foster your own spiritual renewal through wisdom:

1. Daily Meditation and Prayer:

Start each day by dedicating time to meditate on key scriptures such as Proverbs 3:5-6. Ask for guidance to align your heart and mind with divine wisdom. Reflect on areas of your life where change is needed and invite God's presence into your decision-making process.

2. Structured Journaling:

Keep a transformation journal where you record insights, challenges, and steps taken toward personal growth. Reflect on how embracing humility and wisdom has shifted your perspective and helped you overcome adversity. Over time, review your journal for recurring themes and progress.

3. Mentorship and Accountability:

Seek out mentors or join a community group that meets regularly to discuss spiritual growth and ethical living. These relationships can provide necessary correction, encouragement, and inspiration as you navigate your own journey of transformation.

4. Serve Others:

Engage in acts of service, which not only benefit your community but also serve as practical expressions of inner change. Whether through volunteering, sharing your testimony, or simply being a compassionate listener, serving others reinforces the lessons of humility and trust.

5. Reflective Reading and Study:

Regularly study the wisdom literature of the Bible as well as other spiritual texts that resonate with you. In doing so, allow the themes of transformation, renewal, and ethical living to challenge and guide your personal choices.

# Concluding Reflections

The journey toward spiritual transformation through wisdom is both profound and deeply personal. As we have seen in Proverbs 3 and through countless testimonies, acquiring wisdom leads not only to practical benefits in daily life but to an inner transformation—a renewal of the heart and mind that redefines our character and directs us toward a purposeful existence. This transformation is marked by a reordering of priorities, the cultivation of humility, and an openness to both divine correction and human guidance.

The interplay between the heart and mind is at the very core of this process. When we let our hearts be touched by the love and discipline of God, and when our minds are renewed by insights that transcend human limitations, we embark on a journey that reshapes our very identity. History and modern experiences alike affirm that those who embrace this journey are not only better equipped to face life's challenges but often emerge as beacons of hope and exemplars of transformative leadership.

May the insights from this chapter encourage you to take deliberate steps on your own path to transformation. Ask yourself: How can the wisdom of Scripture and the testimonies of those who have gone before guide you to a deeper, more authentic life? Are there areas in your heart and mind that need renewal? And what practical measures can you implement today to foster that transformation?

The call to spiritual transformation through wisdom is an invitation to see life through a new lens—a lens that values humility, ethical living, and an ongoing quest for truth. As you embrace this calling, may you experience a renewed spirit that not only changes your life from within but also radiates outward, touching the lives of those around you.

In summary, biblical wisdom offers a powerful vehicle for change—a pathway to inner renewal, ethical maturity, and lasting fulfillment. The transformation achieved through wisdom is holistic, involving both heart and mind, and is documented in the lives of individuals who, by surrendering to divine guidance, have experienced profound personal growth. Embrace this journey, and allow the transformative power of wisdom to guide you toward a life marked by clarity, purpose, and enduring spiritual abundance.

# Chapter 9: Integrating Proverbs 3 in Contemporary Life

Biblical wisdom has transcended time as an enduring guide for living with purpose, ethics, and balance. Proverbs 3, in particular, offers a rich tapestry of insights that continue to speak to individuals in every era. However, integrating these ancient principles into modern life is not without its challenges. Today's world presents materialism, stress, and moral relativism—forces that can obscure the timeless truths found in Scripture. This chapter explores these challenges and proposes practical strategies for applying the guidance of Proverbs 3 in personal, professional, and community contexts. In addition, it provides discussion prompts for group study and church gatherings to help believers share insights and deepen their collective understanding of biblical wisdom.

## Challenges in the Modern World

### Materialism and the Pursuit of Instant Gratification

In contemporary society, materialism is pervasive. Many find themselves caught in the relentless pursuit of wealth, possessions, and status. Consumer culture and advertising promote the idea that success is measured by what one owns rather than by the quality of one's character or the depth of spiritual conviction. This worldview can stand in stark contrast to Proverbs 3, which advises trust in the Lord over reliance on personal understanding and worldly accumulation.

Materialism leads to a cycle of constant comparison, anxiety, and a focus on short-term gains. The paradox is that as people accumulate more, they can feel increasingly empty. Proverbs 3 reminds us that true security and fulfillment come from acknowledging God in all our ways rather than placing our hope in material wealth. Integrating biblical wisdom in this context means actively resisting the lure of consumerism and developing values that prioritize spiritual well-being over external markers of success.

## Stress and the Pace of Modern Life

Another significant challenge is stress. The modern pace of life—with its high demands in the workplace, digital distractions, and a culture that glorifies busyness—often leaves little time for quiet reflection and spiritual renewal. Many individuals experience chronic stress that affects their emotional, physical, and mental health.

Proverbs 3:5–6 offers a counterpoint to the frantic rhythm of modern living. The admonition to "trust in the LORD with all your heart" calls for a deliberate slowing down, a willingness to rely on divine guidance rather than succumbing to the pressures of self-reliance. Stress management in the modern world requires intentional practices that nurture inner peace and redirect focus from external chaos toward the still, sure foundation of faith.

## Moral Relativism and Ethical Uncertainty

Moral relativism has also emerged as a pervasive cultural trend. In a pluralistic society where values are often seen as subjective, the objective moral standards of the Bible can seem out of step with contemporary ethics. As a result, many struggle with questions about right and wrong, and the clarity of biblical truth may feel diluted amidst competing worldviews.

Proverbs 3, however, presents clear ethical guidelines that are not confined to ancient cultural contexts but continue to resonate with issues of integrity, justice, and compassion today. By anchoring one's life in the promises and principles of Scripture, individuals can find a solid foundation amid the shifting sands of moral ambiguity. Adopting biblical ethics requires conviction and a readiness to resist cultural pressures that favor self-interest over the common good.

# Practical Strategies for Integration

To successfully integrate the principles of Proverbs 3 into contemporary life, one must engage both in internal transformation and in practical, day-to-day applications. The following strategies provide actionable steps for personal, professional, and communal integration.

## Personal Life

## 1. Prioritize Spiritual Practices

- Daily Devotionals and Prayer:

Carve out intentional time each day for prayer and meditation on Proverbs 3:5–6. Reflect on how these verses can guide decisions and counterbalance the distractions of modern life. Consider using a devotional journal to record insights and personal applications.

- Mindfulness and Reflection:

Incorporate mindfulness practices that allow you to pause and re-center throughout the day. Meditation on key verses can help foster a renewed mind and a tranquil spirit, combating the stress and anxiety induced by a fast-paced lifestyle.

### 2. Simplify and Reevaluate Priorities

- Minimalism:

Consider adopting elements of minimalism in your personal life. By reducing the focus on material possessions, you can rechannel energy toward spiritual growth and the nurturing of relationships.

Reflect on how the wisdom of Proverbs calls you to trust in God rather than in the wealth of the world.

- Values Assessment:

Regularly assess your values and goals. Ask yourself: Do my pursuits align with the teachings of biblical wisdom? Are my goals centered on temporary gains or on enduring spiritual and moral richness?

## 3. Embrace Accountability and Community

- Mentorship:

Seek out mentors or spiritual advisors who model a life of integrated wisdom. Their experiences can provide insights and practical advice for navigating challenges, while their accountability can help you remain true to your commitments.

- Small Group Fellowship:

Engage in small group discussions or Bible study groups focused on the wisdom literature. Sharing personal testimonies and insights with like-minded believers creates a supportive environment for growth and accountability.

# Professional Life

## 1. Ethical Leadership and Decision-Making

- Value-Based Management:

In the workplace, integrate the ethics of Proverbs 3 by making decisions based on integrity and fairness rather than solely on profit or personal gain. Ensure that your actions reflect a commitment to trust and transparency.

- Humility in Leadership:

Leaders should model humility by openly acknowledging the contributions of others and remaining receptive to constructive feedback. This approach not only enhances team morale but also cultivates an organizational culture that values ethical behavior and mutual respect.

## 2. Stress Management and Work-Life Balance

- Boundaries and Priorities:
Create clear boundaries between work and personal life. Allocate time for rest, reflection, and spiritual practice. By doing so, you reduce the negative effects of stress and create space for wisdom to shape your decisions.
- Mindful Work Practices:
Introduce mindfulness techniques into your professional routine. Whether through brief meditative breaks or structured reflection sessions, these practices can help you center your thoughts and approach challenges with a calm, clear mind.

## 3. Corporate Social Responsibility

- Ethical Practices:
Advocate for corporate policies that prioritize social responsibility and ethical decision-making. Encourage transparency, fair treatment of employees, and community engagement as integral components of business success.
- Community Investment:
Consider how your professional resources can be used to benefit the broader community. Whether through volunteering, charitable donations, or initiating community projects, contributing to the common good can be a powerful expression of the wisdom found in Proverbs.

# Community Life

## 1. Building Faith-Based Community Initiatives

- Church and Small Groups:

Churches and small groups can serve as incubators for integrating biblical wisdom into community life. Organize study sessions, workshops, or service projects that allow participants to explore the teachings of Proverbs 3 and apply them in tangible ways.

- Local Outreach:

Engage in outreach programs that provide practical support to those in need. Whether through food drives, mentoring programs, or community clean-up initiatives, these efforts embody the ethical and compassionate principles of biblical wisdom.

## 2. Fostering Dialogue and Mentoring

- Intergenerational Dialogues:

Initiate conversations between different generations within your community. Older members can share how biblical wisdom transformed their lives, while younger individuals can offer fresh perspectives on applying these teachings in today's world. Such dialogues promote mutual learning and strengthen community bonds.

- Peer Mentoring:

Establish peer mentoring programs that enable individuals to share their personal journeys and insights. This approach not only reinforces accountability but also creates a network where spiritual growth is collectively nurtured.

## 3. Educational Programs and Workshops

- Bible Studies and Seminars:

Host educational programs focused on the wisdom literature, particularly Proverbs 3. Workshops can offer both theological insights and practical applications, discussing topics such as ethical leadership, stress management, and balancing material pursuits with spiritual growth.

- Discussion Forums:

Create forums for open discussion on issues like moral relativism, materialism, and contemporary challenges. Facilitating dialogue helps community members explore how biblical wisdom can offer clarity and direction in complex situations.

# Group Discussion and Study Questions

To deepen understanding and enrich the application of biblical wisdom, engaging in group discussions is essential. Below are several discussion prompts and study questions that can guide small groups, church gatherings, or community forums. These questions are designed to encourage thoughtful reflection, share personal experiences, and foster a deeper communal understanding of Proverbs 3.

## Discussion Prompts

1. Trust versus Self-Reliance:

- How do you personally navigate the tension between trusting in God and relying on your own understanding in daily life?

- Can you share a specific instance when choosing to trust God rather than your own judgment led to a meaningful outcome?

2. Materialism and True Prosperity:

- In what ways does modern consumer culture challenge the biblical view of prosperity as described in Proverbs 3?

- How can we cultivate a perspective that values spiritual wealth over material accumulation?

3. Managing Stress Through Faith:

- What practical steps have you taken to manage stress and maintain balance in your life?

- How has your faith helped you reclaim peace during times of high pressure and uncertainty?

4. Integrating Ethical Principles in the Workplace:

- For those in professional settings, what are some challenges you face in upholding ethical standards?

- How can leaders and employees create environments that reflect the values promoted in Proverbs 3?

5. Community and Accountability:

- In what ways have community groups or church activities supported your spiritual growth?

- How can accountability partners or mentorship relationships be strengthened within your local context?

## Reflective Study Questions

1. Personal Reflection on Biblical Principles:

- Reflect on Proverbs 3:5-6. What does it mean to "trust in the LORD with all your heart" in your current life situation?

- How can acknowledging God in all your ways transform your decision-making process?

2. Reexamining Priorities:

- Identify areas in your life where material pursuits have taken precedence over spiritual growth.

- What concrete steps can you take to reorient your priorities in light of the wisdom found in Proverbs 3?

3. Ethical Challenges:

- Consider a recent ethical dilemma you encountered. How did you apply (or how could you have applied) the principles of Proverbs 3 to resolve it?

- What long-term impact might the consistent application of these principles have on your character and relationships?

4. Group Application:

- As a group, discuss practical ways your community could become a living example of biblical wisdom.

- What initiatives could be implemented to help members of your community better integrate these teachings into their lives?

5. Future Planning:

- What habits or practices would you like to develop over the next six months that reflect the teachings of Proverbs 3?

- How will you measure the impact of these changes on your personal growth and on your community?

## Moving Forward: Embracing a Life Directed by Divine Wisdom

Integrating Proverbs 3 into contemporary life is both a personal commitment and a communal endeavor. As we have seen, modern challenges—materialism, stress, and moral relativism—pose significant obstacles to living in accordance with biblical principles. Yet, these challenges also provide opportunities for reinvention and growth. By embracing practical strategies and engaging in community dialogue, believers can transform modern hurdles into stepping stones toward a richer, more meaningful life.

The integration of biblical wisdom requires us to be intentional. It calls for daily practices that reaffirm our trust in God, recalibrate our priorities, and reshape our interactions within our family, workplace, and broader community. Whether through personal journaling, mindfulness practices, or active participation in faith-based groups, the process of integrating Proverbs 3 is dynamic and continuous.

Moreover, the discussions and study questions provided in this chapter serve as catalysts for collective insight. As individuals share their experiences and challenges, they create an environment where biblical wisdom is lived out authentically. This communal exchange not only reinforces personal growth but also strengthens the bonds of faith, creating a network of accountability, support, and shared purpose.

In conclusion, integrating Proverbs 3 into contemporary life is not merely about acquiring knowledge—it is about transforming how we live. It is an invitation to shift our focus from fleeting, material success to enduring, spiritual fulfillment. It challenges us to trust deeply, to act ethically, and to serve compassionately amid the complex landscape of modern culture.

May this chapter serve as both a guide and an inspiration for anyone seeking to live a life imbued with the transformative power of divine wisdom. By embracing the practical strategies outlined herein, engaging in reflective group discussions, and committing to personal growth, you can begin to see that the ancient truths of Proverbs 3 remain profoundly relevant today. In doing so, you join a timeless tradition—a tradition that bridges the gap between the ancient and the modern, directing your paths, enriching your relationships, and ultimately, shaping a legacy of wisdom for generations to come.

# Chapter 10: Conclusion and Devotional Guide for Continued Growth

The journey through the teachings of Proverbs 3 and the broader study of biblical wisdom has been one marked by challenges, discoveries, and profound personal insights. This concluding chapter brings together the key insights explored throughout the study guide, offers a roadmap for a personal journey of continued growth, and provides devotional tools—including reflective questions, prayers, and meditations—to solidify a lifelong relationship with wisdom and God. In addition, we present recommended resources for further exploration of biblical wisdom, encouraging you to continue this transformative journey.

## Synthesis of Key Insights

### The Foundational Role of Wisdom

At the heart of our exploration is the understanding that biblical wisdom is not merely an accumulation of intellectual knowledge but a transformative, living principle that reorients our entire being. Proverbs 3 reminds us that true wisdom begins with a humble trust in the Lord. The recurring themes—trust, humility, ethical living, and the interplay between divine correction and personal growth—serve as a blueprint for integrating spiritual insight into every facet of life.

- Trust and Surrender:

From the opening verses that implore us to "Trust in the LORD with all your heart" to the promise that "He shall direct your paths," we learn that surrendering our self-reliance and acknowledging God in every decision is the gateway to divine guidance.

- Humility as a Virtue:

Humility emerged as the cornerstone of both spiritual transformation and material as well as emotional prosperity. Recognizing that our own understanding is limited encourages us to remain open to correction, thereby paving the way for genuine growth.

- Ethical Living and Corrective Discipline:

Discipline and correction, when viewed through the lens of divine love, are not punitive but restorative. Embracing divine discipline is essential to foster resilience and moral clarity. It is through correction that we refine our character and evolve into embodiments of wisdom.

- Integration of Heart and Mind:

The study has shown that the renewal of the heart—through love, compassion, and humility—and the renewal of the mind—through discernment and learning—are inseparable. Their harmonious interplay is pivotal to the transformation of character.

## The Path to Personal and Communal Transformation

The transformative power of biblical wisdom extends beyond personal growth to foster enhanced relationships, ethical leadership, and community flourishing. The lessons of Proverbs 3 resonate in every sphere of life:

- Personal Transformation:

Engaging with biblical wisdom transforms not only our thought processes but also our emotions and priorities. We come to value integrity over material wealth and discover that inner peace and purpose are achieved by aligning our lives with the divine will.

- Professional and Ethical Leadership:

In the workplace, the principles of honesty, humility, and service guide ethical decision-making. Leaders who internalize these values create environments that foster trust, collaboration, and long-term prosperity.

- Community and Accountability:

When communities collectively embrace the wisdom of Scripture, the result is a culture of support, shared growth, and mutual accountability. Whether through small groups, church gatherings, or mentorship programs, the integration of biblical wisdom strengthens bonds and nurtures a spirit of communal care.

## Lifelong Learning and Continued Growth

Perhaps the most important insight is that the pursuit of wisdom is not a destination but a lifelong journey. Every challenge and correction serves as an opportunity to deepen our understanding and renew our commitment to living in harmony with divine truth. The study guide has provided tools, reflective practices, and discussion questions that are designed not only for academic inquiry but for practical, everyday application. As you continue on this path, remember that the transformative power of wisdom is ongoing; it is revealed gradually through persistent seeking, humble reflection, and a willingness to be continually reshaped by God's love.

# A Personal Journey Forward

## Integrating Lessons into Daily Living

The insights from this study are meant to be practical and applicable in every area of your life. Here are several steps to help you integrate these lessons:

1. Commit to Daily Devotions:

Develop a routine of daily prayer, meditation, and scripture reading. Begin each day by reciting key verses such as Proverbs 3:5–6, and allow these words to set your tone. Let these passages remind you to surrender your worries, trust in divine guidance, and reorient your decisions.

2. Cultivate Humility and Openness:

Actively work on developing humility. Accept that you will make mistakes and that correction is a catalyst for improvement. Embrace feedback from both divine inspiration and your community. Reflect on moments when acknowledging your limitations led to breakthroughs in understanding and personal growth.

3. Practice Reflective Journaling:

Keep a journal dedicated to your spiritual journey. Record insights, challenges, corrections, and moments of divine intervention. Use this journal to document your progress, set personal goals, and review how the lessons of Proverbs have influenced your decisions and relationships.

4. Engage in Community and Accountability:

Join or form small groups, Bible study circles, or accountability partnerships. Sharing your journey with others not only provides encouragement but also creates a network of support that reinforces the principles of trust, obedience, and ethical living.

5. Embrace Correction as a Positive Force:

Reframe experiences of correction and discipline as opportunities for growth. When faced with setbacks, consider them as divine nudges steering you in a direction that leads to greater wisdom. Reflect on your responses to challenges and identify how these experiences have refined your character.

## Shaping Your Future with Wisdom

Your journey toward wisdom is deeply personal, yet it is part of a greater tapestry of faith that spans generations. As you look forward, consider how you might:

- Revise Your Goals:

Align your personal, professional, and spiritual goals with the values of wisdom. Focus not solely on measurable achievements but on the cultivation of character, integrity, and compassion.

- Influence Others:

As your understanding deepens, become a mentor or a leader in your community. Share the insights you've gained through this study, and help others discover the transformative power of embracing biblical wisdom.

- Stay Curious and Committed:

Remain dedicated to lifelong learning. Continue to explore biblical texts, attend workshops or seminars, and read further on the themes of wisdom, humility, and spiritual transformation. Let your desire for growth guide you through all life's seasons.

# Prayer and Reflection

## Guided Prayers

Prayer is a powerful tool for internalizing and acting upon the truths found in Scripture. Use the following prayers as a starting point for your daily devotional practice:

Morning Prayer:

"Heavenly Father, as I begin this day, I open my heart to Your wisdom. Help me to trust You with all my heart, to lean not on my own understanding, and to acknowledge You in every decision I make. Renew my spirit, guide my steps, and fill me with the peace that comes from Your presence. Amen."

Midday Reflection:

"Lord, in the midst of my busy day, remind me of Your constant care. When stress arises and my own strength falters, help me to find rest in Your guidance. May Your wisdom shine through my thoughts and actions. Guide me to treat others with kindness, empathy, and respect. Amen."

Evening Meditation:

"Gracious God, as I close this day, I reflect on the lessons learned and the moments of correction that have shaped me. Thank You for Your patience and for the divine discipline that molds me into a better person. Grant me the wisdom to rest in Your truth and the courage to rise again with renewed purpose tomorrow. Amen."

## Reflective Questions and Meditation Points

Use these questions as anchors for your personal reflection time:

1. Trust and Surrender:

- What does it mean to trust in the Lord with all your heart?

- Can you identify recent moments when surrendering control led to positive outcomes?

2. Embracing Correction:

- How have challenges or corrections in your life prompted growth or a deeper understanding of God's purpose for you?

- In what ways can you shift your perspective to view correction as an act of divine love?

3. Renewal of Heart and Mind:

- Which areas of your life most need renewal and transformation?

- Reflect on a moment when a change in perspective transformed your actions or relationships. What was the outcome?

4. Community and Accountability:

- How can sharing your journey with others help reinforce your commitment to living wisely?

- Consider the ways in which your community has influenced your spiritual growth. How can this be strengthened?

5. Vision for the Future:

- What practical steps can you take in the coming weeks to integrate the lessons of Proverbs 3 more fully into your life?

- How can you measure your progress and stay accountable to your goals?

## Meditation on Proverbs 3:5-6

Spend a few minutes each day in quiet meditation on these verses:

"Trust in the LORD with all your heart, and lean not on your own understanding; in all your ways acknowledge Him, and He shall direct your paths."

Visualize yourself walking along a path illuminated by divine light. Imagine that each step is guided by God's loving hand, easing the burdens of uncertainty and stress. With each breath, internalize the truth that You are not alone—that God is directing your life with purpose and care. Let this imagery fill you with calm and resolve for the day ahead.

# Additional Resources for Continued Exploration

To further enrich your understanding of biblical wisdom and to continue your spiritual growth, consider exploring these recommended resources:

## Books

- "The Book of Proverbs" by Derek Kidner:

A highly accessible commentary that delves into the historical, cultural, and theological dimensions of Proverbs, offering practical insights that are applicable to modern living.

- "The Wisdom of God" by John Eldredge:

This book weaves together personal experiences with biblical insights, encouraging readers to see God's presence in every facet of life.

- "Living by the Book" by Howard G. Hendricks and William D. Hendricks:

An excellent resource for understanding how to apply biblical teachings in daily life through careful study, practical advice, and reflective questions.

Online Resources

-Bible Study Tools and Commentaries:

Websites such as [BibleGateway](https://www.biblegateway.com) and [Blue Letter Bible](https://www.blueletterbible.org) offer a wealth of commentaries, translations, and study materials to deepen your understanding of Proverbs 3 and related scriptures.

- Faith-Based Podcasts and Online Sermons:

Engage with podcasts or sermons that focus on biblical wisdom, spiritual growth, and ethical living. Many churches and Christian organizations produce regular content that can inspire and challenge your current perspectives.

- Interactive Bible Study Platforms:

Platforms such as [RightNow Media](https://www.rightnowmedia.org) provide video studies and group discussions that help integrate biblical principles into contemporary contexts, offering both academic insight and practical application.

## Community and Mentorship

- Local Church Groups and Study Circles:

Participate in or organize small groups focused on the wisdom literature of the Bible. Sharing experiences and insights in community can greatly enhance your understanding and application of these principles.

- Mentorship Programs:

Look for mentorship opportunities within your church or community where you can either serve as a mentor or benefit from the guidance of someone who has walked the path of wisdom before you.

# Final Thoughts

The call to continued growth is a lifelong invitation—a journey that does not end with the closing of this study guide but continues each day as you strive to live a life rooted in divine wisdom. Proverbs 3 remains a timeless guide, offering clarity in the midst of modern challenges, encouraging ethical action, and promising the blessings of inner peace, ethical strength, and spiritual renewal.

Remember that the journey toward wisdom is as much about the everyday small decisions as it is about major life changes. Each act of trust, every moment of humility, and every instance of embracing correction contributes to your transformation. As you integrate these lessons into your life, you join a long legacy of believers who have found that true success is measured not by what we possess, but by how deeply we are connected to the divine purpose that guides all things.

May you continue this journey with a heart open to divine guidance, a mind receptive to growth, and a spirit emboldened by the love and wisdom of God. Use the reflective practices, prayers, and discussions provided here to anchor your progress, and let your life be a living testimony to the transformative power of biblical wisdom.

In closing, let this chapter be a reminder that your spiritual growth is a dynamic, ongoing process. Each day brings new opportunities to learn, to be corrected, and to renew your commitment to living according to the truth found in Scripture. With unwavering trust and a humble heart, step forward into the future, knowing that the wisdom of Proverbs 3 will continue to light your path and shape your journey—today, tomorrow, and for all the days to come.

# Don't miss out!

Visit the website below and you can sign up to receive emails whenever Sister Felicity Rivera publishes a new book. There's no charge and no obligation.

https://books2read.com/r/B-A-XTBRD-GWCFG

**BOOKS 2 READ**

Connecting independent readers to independent writers.

# About the Author

Sister Felicity Rivera blends liturgical studies with pastoral experience to craft inclusive Bible study guides. Her writings, enriched with historical anecdotes and social insights, illuminate timeless scriptural lessons for modern, diverse communities.

www.ingramcontent.com/pod-product-compliance
Lightning Source LLC
Chambersburg PA
CBHW051226160726
47994CB00002B/762